WALKING THE HIGH DESERT

WALKING THE HIGH DESERT

ENCOUNTERS WITH RURAL AMERICA ALONG THE OREGON DESERT TRAIL

ELLEN WATERSTON

UNIVERSITY OF WASHINGTON PRESS

Seattle

Design by Katrina Noble
Composed in Scala, typeface designed by Martin Majoor
Map by Greg Cross

24   23   22   21   5   4   3   2

Printed and bound in the United States of America

UNIVERSITY OF WASHINGTON PRESS
uwapress.uw.edu

LIBRARY OF CONGRESS CATALOGING-IN-PUBLICATION DATA
Names: Waterston, Ellen, author.
Title: Walking the High Desert : Encounters with rural America along the
    Oregon Desert Trail / Ellen Waterston.
Description: Seattle : University of Washington Press, [2020] | Includes biblio-
    graphical references and index.
Identifiers: LCCN 2019046574 (print) | LCCN 2019046575 (ebook) |
    ISBN 9780295747507 (paperback) | ISBN 9780295747514 (ebook)
Subjects: LCSH: Oregon Desert Trail (Or.) | Oregon, Eastern—Description
    and travel. | Oregon, Central—Description and travel. | High Desert (Or.)—
    Description and travel.
Classification: LCC F882.O54 W38 2020 (print) | LCC F882.O54 (ebook) |
    DDC 917.95/9304—dc23
LC record available at https://lccn.loc.gov/2019046574
LC ebook record available at https://lccn.loc.gov/2019046575

To my grandchildren Samuel, Elijah, and Amalia

CONTENTS

THE OREGON DESERT TRAIL

Bend

BADLANDS WILDERNESS

Central Oregon Volcanics

97

Pine Mountain

20

31

Fort Rock

Christmas Valley

Summer Lake

West Basin and Range

Paisley

395

Oregon

Area of detail

Plush

Lakeview

140

395

Adel

MILES

0   25   50

395

Burns

Malheur National Wildlife Refuge

78

205

East Basin and Range

Frenchglen

Hart Mtn. National Antelope Refuge

Andrews

Fields

Steens Mountain Wilderness

Pueblo Mountains

Trout Creek Mountains

26   84

Ontario

20

LAKE OWYHEE STATE PARK

Rome

95

Owyhee Canyonlands

95

IDAHO

CALIFORNIA   NEVADA

PREFACE

I have often speculated that if every student was given one thing—an eraser, a bird's nest, a wad of clay—and asked over the course of their schooling to learn everything about that one thing—chemical structure, origin, history—an entire education could be had. So it is with the high desert. Forget kindergarten. All you ever needed to know can be learned from Oregon's high desert: your person, your place, your thing. To paraphrase writer and naturalist Joseph Krutch, it is usually in the middle of a desert or on the top of a mountain that the vision comes or the test is met. The high desert has both. That this little-known area of the United States should touch on so much of what is at the forefront of national concern is amazing (how do it know?), convenient (for the purposes of this book), and sad. Sad because this trusting, naïve, earnest, stubbly, grumpy old man of a desert is not spared from these big issues that are impacting even the most remote of locations. Sad because we have had ample opportunity to address them before, in other places, and have not.

Walking the High Desert is divided into four two-hundred-mile sections, give or take: Central Oregon Volcanics, West Basin and Range, East Basin and Range, and the Owyhee Canyonlands. Each is named after the most distinguishing geographic characteristic of that stretch of the Oregon Desert Trail (ODT), which meanders for

750 miles from the Oregon Badlands Wilderness outside of Bend to the Owyhee Canyonlands near Rome.

The chapters within each section focus on specific places along the trail and on issues seemingly unique to those locations. But not so fast. On closer examination, what becomes clear is that regionally and nationally the issues are strikingly similar and familiar, as is the response to them. When it comes to any sort of solution, it appears we are high-centered, wheels off the ground, going nowhere fast, or as cowboys ingloriously describe it when a cow lands on her back in an irrigation ditch, we're tits up. The same urgent concerns have, like invasive weeds, colonized almost every living room, backyard, town, city, and region. The compelling contradictory cases being made on all sides of all issues parade confidently and persuasively across the editorial pages, farms, rivers, forests, lakes, and deserts of our existence. No coming together or resolution seems possible. Indeed, as the trajectory of this narrative crescendos at the Malheur National Wildlife Refuge, the future of the region and nation appears very bleak indeed, the situation dire.

After nearly eight hundred challenging miles, the trail ends inside the embrace of the magnificent Owyhee Canyonlands of southeastern Oregon. What better place to reflect on the journey just taken than surrounded by the beauty of Leslie Gulch's rhyolite canyon walls and spires. What that moment of reflection reveals is the invitation to look at how you think, whoever you are, at where you live, wherever that might be, through the optic of the high desert of southeastern Oregon. This thru-hike kicks up all kinds of stalemates and bad news, it's true, but also unanticipated answers to issues that grind away both in the high desert and far from its arid climes. Large and small examples of genuine collaboration encountered along the trek make their way to the surface, pushing aside all the no can dos. What better place than Leslie Gulch to gather those hopeful examples into a bouquet of rationality and aspiration. Indeed, when all is said and done, this is a journey across "the geography of hope," as Wallace Stegner described the arid West. In the end, *Walking the High Desert* provides prescriptions for opposing sides to come together, to create consensus to propel us forward no matter where in the who or the what we are.

I have a cocktail party theory. If I leave with one thought- or action-provoking exchange, it was time well spent. If one line, one paragraph, one chapter of this book proves to be that exchange; if everyone reading is cajoled, inspired, or offended into positive reflection and action, then this has been a party worth attending. Embedded in the questions this book poses is an urgent petition to us all to put all four wheels on the ground and head out, shoulder to shoulder, to find new ways to understand and reimagine our relationship to the environment and to one another.

WALKING THE HIGH DESERT

CENTRAL OREGON VOLCANICS

Warning: The ODT is an extremely challenging route for the thru-hiker, both physically and logistically. Travelers on the ODT need to be aware of the remoteness, lack of cell communication and environmental hazards. There are several potentially dry stretches with no reliable water, and water caching ahead of time is necessary. Thru-hiking the entire trail is not for the beginning long-distance hiker. Similarly, those traveling shorter lengths of the trail also need to be fully prepared and aware of the challenges of the ODT.

OREGON DESERT TRAIL GUIDEBOOK

ONE

High Centered

FIRST OF ALL, it's "Orygun," not "Orahgone." And it's "Malhyure" out here. Not the French pronunciation "Mal-uhr," although the French trappers who came through Oregon's high desert in 1819 were plenty unhappy. Once they left the stands of ponderosa in the mountains and entered the desert, nothing went right. Their cached beaver pelts were snatched by Indians. There was little water, no shelter, no shade. It didn't go much better for the Hawaiian trappers working for the North West Company who came up missing the same year in the farthest southeastern corner of the Oregon Territory and after whom the stunningly beautiful Owyhee River and Canyonlands were named, that being the standard spelling of Hawaii at the time.

Speaking of names, the Oregon Outback, the sage steppe, the empty quarter, the cold desert, the back of beyond, cowboy country, the nothing-but-nothing, the sagebrush ocean, the Great Basin, the great sandy desert, the rolling sage plain, the Artemisia desert all refer to the same thing: the high desert. Since the nineteenth century, us settlers have tried to name this place and thereby, as is the fancy of settlers, to lay claim to it. But the enduring fascination of the high desert, and the reason its survival as a wild place is within reach, may well lie in the fact that this vast open can't quite be named. It stays always one step ahead of the namers, luring us who would try deeper and deeper into its embrace.

People start to channel their inner Carlos Castaneda after spending time in this high desert. They also get real. That a rancher hangs a coyote hide on a fence doesn't mean the rancher is angry at the government, as environmental historian Nancy Langston speculated in a January 6, 2016, *New York Times* op-ed. It means the rancher is angry at the coyote. Sometimes a cigar is just a cigar. The coyote ate the rancher's newborn livestock. "Makes a person mad," states a rancher in typically understated fashion. The only indication of a stronger emotion: the force behind the spit of chewing tobacco he sends to the ground. As far as the rancher is concerned, the dead coyote draped over the barbed wire fence murdered, robbed, and ate a hole in his wallet.

This brief pronunciation and cultural sensitivity guide matters. Simply stated, we must remove our cultural and class filters to have the necessary conversation about this place and about all the people who love it in their unique and seemingly incompatible ways.

Those who have never been to Oregon imagine the whole state rainy and green, like Portland or Seattle, and believe that the *Portlandia* culture made popular by the sketch comedy television series characterizes all ninety-eight thousand square miles of this northwestern wonderland. In fact, three-quarters of the state is dry and separated from "the valley," as the western portion is referred to, by the majestic High Cascades, all dormant volcanoes, at least for now.

They block the rains from coming east, keep the high desert the high desert. Where I live, in Bend, at the foot of the Cascades on the eastern side, the average annual rainfall is twelve inches a year. As one old-timer said: "Remember that time it rained forty days and forty nights? We got an inch and a half in eastern Oregon." It's a part of the world where evaporation exceeds precipitation literally and metaphorically, giving back more than it receives. It's a desert that doesn't get the credit it deserves for its generosity.

In April of 2016 I drove the 130 miles east and south from Bend, located roughly in the middle of the state, to Burns to take part in the annual Harney County Migratory Bird Festival, a favorite event of mine. So good to get away from Bend's increasingly California-like culture. A former lumber mill town, Bend is now ultrachic, latte'd, churning with construction and growth, and teeming with self-aware forty-something bio- and high-tech CEOs. One of the fastest-growing communities in the United States, it boasts a populace remarkably unaware of the desert that surrounds them. Perhaps that's good news for the high desert.

Lucky for me it's only a matter of driving a short distance east until I am reunited with what has become my reassurance that all is right with the world: vast sagebrush flats, the echo of what used to be ocean bottom, flanked by escarpments and buttes, gnarled juniper forests, basalt canyons carved by ancient rivers. Other than power lines, and perhaps the distant silhouette of a barn or ranch house, nothing interrupts the view. Along Highway 20 between Bend and Burns, if you stop by the side of the road in the spring, the loudest sound is likely the buzzing of a fly. Artist Robert Dahl, who serves on the advisory council of Bend's High Desert Museum, once placed a cheesy aluminum folding chair with nylon webbing in the middle of Highway 20 and sat down for the ultimate selfie and existential

Christmas card: nothingness ahead, nothingness on either side, nothing to recommend going in any direction . . . or not.

Closer to Burns the palette changes from the muted browns, grays, and ochres of the sage to bright green, evidence of spring melt and a water table that sits just below the surface of the miles and miles of pancake-flat fields. Dramatically framing them to the south is the 9,733-foot, snowcapped Steens Mountain, its southernmost side a dramatic escarpment that plummets to the Alvord Desert before sliding into base in Nevada. Ranch houses in Burns that are built on these seasonally soggy paddy flats don't have basements. Abandoned homesteads and barns shrug their way to the earth as their underpinnings rot. The spring runoff in this landlocked basin creates perfect habitat for birds . . . and the word has spread.

The area is part of the migratory path for a huge variety of large- and small-winged victories. Birders with binoculars cruise along the dykes that frame fields of hay, alfalfa, and Timothy grass, training their eyes on yellow-headed blackbirds, bitterns, meadowlarks, mergansers, egrets, and willets. Visitors learn to return the favor of an index finger lifted off the steering wheel by the rancher as they pass his oncoming pickup, his stock dog leaning into the wind, teetering on bales of hay stacked in the bed of the truck. It feels like acceptance into the fraternity of those who work the land for a living. It used to be most of us could recall a relative who farmed or ranched. Not so much anymore.

What started in 1981 in the town's grange hall, the Harney County Migratory Bird Festival now locates activities all over Burns and at favorite viewpoints within the 187,000 acres of the Malheur National Wildlife Refuge, with bird talks and guided tours held within the refuge and on adjacent ranches. You're likely to see flocks of snow geese lifting off the greening meadows like bedsheets flapping in the wind, clusters of avocets and phalaropes probing the marshes and irrigated fields for food, squadrons of haughty white pelicans, and sandhill cranes looking as regal and prehistoric as they are, their ungainly squawk matching their ungainly stride. What people come to observe and exalt is beautiful, glorious, fragile.

On the Saturday night of the festival a dinner is held at the Harney County Fairgrounds. In 2016 there looked to be two hundred people in attendance. More? In any case, a record-breaking turnout, according to organizers. Long banquet tables were decorated with rough-hewn barnwood boxes made by local high school students and filled with wildflowers. Crude paintings of birds, also by students, were on display to be auctioned as well as raffle items, from carved ducks to horsehair bracelets to homemade apple butter crafted by local artists and cooks. The gregarious organizer, president of the Burns Chamber of Commerce (considering all the empty storefronts in town, a triumph of hope), orchestrated the evening skillfully as she called out raffle winners and introduced speakers. The dinner was prepared by members of the local Mennonite community. Between the main course and dessert the Mennonite men and boys in their pressed white shirts, the women and girls in their long skirts and small bonnets came out of the kitchen and lined up next to the toiling coffeepots to sing in the purest of harmonies: "When hay is fresh and new, all my praise to You. When hay is fresh and new, all my praise to You."

Presentations featured a talk about sage grouse habitat and the prospect of the bird being protected, a touchy subject among ranchers who fear the designation of the sage grouse as an endangered species will reduce their grazing permits and, therefore, their ability to make a livelihood. For the time being, an uneasy peace had been negotiated between government land-use agencies and private landowners who collaborated successfully to protect existing and create new habitat for the bird. The next talk, by the wife of a local rancher, informed the city folk in attendance about what was happening on ranches in the spring of the year—calving, weaning, haying— and then, clearly off-message, she kind of reared up and declared that, by golly, she supported her community law enforcement officials and the local government land management agencies. Harney County had recently and unintentionally made national headlines due to, let's just say, land-use conflicts and, like the sage grouse issue, also a sensitive topic among locals.

But no matter. No one was inclined to take issue with anything tonight. Nope. If the noisy chatter was any indication, the crowd was clearly eager for a time-out from recent controversies, a night out. Strangers introduced themselves to tablemates, ranchers and visitors applauded anything and everything, knocking their water glasses onto the decorative paper doilies, into their whipped cream and fruit salad. A good time.

My drive to the bird festival that weekend not only took me across an ancient ocean bed framed by exquisite small canyons but paralleled sections of what was christened in 2012 as the Oregon Desert Trail. The Oregon Natural Desert Association (ONDA) plotted and pieced together this 750-mile trail that starts at the Oregon Badlands Wilderness outside of Bend and continues to the southeastern Oregon canyonlands that flank the Owyhee River. Other than a few permitted easements across private land, the trail takes pains to stay on public lands the whole way.

I moved from New England to the high desert to ranch four decades ago. Though I now live in town, my love of this hardscrabble outback still informs my every day. So no surprise that this new trail spoke to me, lured me back into the desert. No longer actively ranching, I decided I would walk sections of the trail and write about it—about what I saw and those I encountered. I would make a point of evenly and fairly presenting the conflicting points of view about repurposing open areas of public land. I prided myself that in so many ways I already knew the players: ranchers; Bureau of Land Management, Forest Service, and Fish and Wildlife employees; schoolteachers in rural schoolhouses; merchants in remote outposts; American Indians on reservations in the high desert; law enforcement officials who, some years back, were kind enough to wave me on, despite my excessive speed, as I made my way along desolate Highway 20 back to the ranch with a station wagon full of fussy infants and sacks of groceries. I knew and understood desert dwellers. This narrative would be about and with them.

At dinner, I asked those at my table their thoughts about ONDA's trail through this wide-open, tumble-dry, high desert. As they finished their salad course and passed around the fresh-baked rolls, I posited my idea that the trail is as long and circuitous as it is not only to lead trekkers through some of the most scenic, and heretofore unexplored, areas of the high desert but also because it dares not stray off public lands lest it create conflicts with private landowners. Did they agree? I wanted to follow, I explained, the course of this high-desert *camino* that skirts key concerns facing this sagebrush ocean: protection of sacred Native American ground, protection of habitat for endangered species, elimination of "predators," "wild" horse protection, grazing "rights" for livestock, hunting "rights," water "rights," demand for recreational land for motorized vehicles, demand for land for what was touted as low-impact recreational uses. I told them I wanted to show how these issues meet head-on at various intersections along the trail. How solutions that work for all are elusive, charged, and complicated but do exist. How, to me, the Oregon Desert

Trail, as it zigs and zags assiduously avoiding privately held tracts, is a powerful metaphor for all the land-use and other issues facing not just southeastern Oregon but all of the ranching West.

As my mashed potatoes and roast beef got cold, I went on (and on . . .). I explained the broader philosophical musings the trail excited in me as suggested by the contradictory rights various groups and users claim. What is wild? Who says grazing is a right? Who says it isn't? What is the highest best use of public lands? According to whom? Whose narrative is most compelling and is influencing policy decisions? Their answers and related questions would be an important part of the book I planned.

Hiking emblematic sections of the Oregon Desert Trail, I explained, I'd also interview other key individuals like them who represent the variety of perspectives on high-desert land use. I'd welcome the questions the process raised and would embrace the conundrum that a passionate love of the same place is not a predictor for common solutions. From these many conversations I would glean reasonable, collaborative approaches to pending decisions. Everyone really *can* just get along. What did they think? No surprise, the varied and compelling responses from my tablemates at the festival dinner, and from those I interviewed subsequently, charted the course for this linked narrative and populated the pages to follow.

This time I'd come to the Migratory Bird Festival with not only my bird book but also walking sticks in hand. My plan was to explore the sections of the Oregon Desert Trail that wind through Harney County before heading back to Bend. Maybe take the festival-sponsored tour through the Malheur National Wildlife Refuge. But this time was different. Most of the birding tours had sold out for the first time in the thirty-four-year history of the festival. The Saturday night banquet was at capacity. Motels were chockablock full. Why?

Because curiosity killed the cat. Because Burns, Oregon, is the county seat of Harney County, where the occupation of the Malheur Wildlife Refuge took place in January and February 2016. It was now April. Ammon Bundy and his band had left the refuge only two months earlier. The buildings they occupied on the refuge and portions of the refuge itself were still closed to the public. Damage to refuge structures, to Northern Paiute artifacts and burial sites was still being assessed. Burns was now on the map. The occupation had identified a new 1 percent—those in the nation who had actually *heard* of Harney County, the refuge, and Burns, Oregon. But, United States of America, ignore what took place there at your peril.

The forty-one-day occupation rendered my original concept for this desert trek narrative a nursery rhyme, la, la, la, a polite conversation about land-use conflicts. The trail was now a mere contrivance to link the perspectives of those who want to harvest natural resources and those who want to protect land for various recreational and environmental reasons. The land-use policy options I intended to write about turned into a shouting match during the occupation between, for starters, those who want no government intrusion and those who understand the benefits of government involvement and collaboration. And since the Bundy occupation, militias have gone public, brother has armed against brother, false information has been embraced as fact. How armed and dangerous we are! How blunt an instrument our thinking has become! How very afraid we are. How misappropriated by the Bundys and their constituents are the United States constitution and, for that matter, God and his son. How misunderstood the laws affecting land-use and, well, everything if one believes the Bundys. And many do.

This unknown region of the United States suddenly became the poster child not only for land-use and conservation issues but for the angry, gun-toting disenfranchised and the rural silent minority who, in combination, helped define the 2016 presidential election, dramatically reframing America's conversation. This demographic, like this area of the United States, is no longer unknown or uncharted. The failure of those—who see themselves as educated and informed, who are at the helm of this nation—to acknowledge and engage the predominantly white, no-longer-silent disenfranchised as much shapes this book as does the elaborate cursive script the Oregon Desert Trail inscribes across southeastern Oregon.

"When hay is fresh and new, all my praise to You. When hay is fresh and new, all my praise to You."

TWO

Insomnia

IT JUST GOES to show how dangerous a sleepless night can be. Brent Fenty claims the notion of creating the Oregon Desert Trail (ODT) came to him during a bout of insomnia in 2010. He didn't wake up with visions of the Bo tree or stone tablets. Rather, he relates, as he stared at the cracks in the ceiling, he imagined a hike he'd like to do through the desert he loves and making it available for others. The reverie combined old roads, existing trails, and cross-country routes, immersing hikers in the territory the Oregon Natural Desert Association has been striving for decades to connect and protect. At the time Fenty was thirty-six years old and had been the executive director of the Bend-based ONDA for three years, a position he held until 2018, when he shifted his role to leading the organization's recently established Oregon Desert Land Trust. Joining forces with the new ONDA executive director, Ryan Houston, the two are working to achieve ONDA's ambitious vision to conserve eight million acres of public lands for current and future generations.

When Fenty speaks of the Oregon Desert Trail staying, for the most part, on public lands, he is referring primarily to those administered by the Bureau of Land Management (BLM). The precursor of that agency was the General Land Office, created in 1812 within the Department of the Treasury to oversee the survey and sale of public domain lands. (It's worth noting that wars between Native Americans and the United States government, which represented land-grabbing white settlers, were ongoing in the Great Basin area into the 1870s.)

By 1930 the Department of the Interior had handed off all the public lands it could to state and private ownership. The glaring and sizable exception was public land remaining unclaimed in the rural West, code for land no white settler wanted other than ranchers who used it for grazing livestock. Efforts to lure homesteaders onto unclaimed acreage began with the 1862 Homestead Act, signed by President Abraham Lincoln, and persisted through the Stock-Raising Homestead Act of 1916 that enabled ranchers to acquire and own a full section of land (640 acres) for their ranch headquarters with adjacent grazing lands still unregulated and used on a first-come, first-served basis. The first-come, first-served part quickly proved to be a recipe for disaster. In response, the 1934 Taylor Grazing Act was accomplished to "prevent harm to public lands due to over-grazing and soil deterioration" but also to protect and stabilize the cattle industry.

The Grazing Service, similar in concept to the Forest Service but specific to rangelands, was created to help address this oil (prevent harm) and water (protect and stabilize the cattle industry) mandate. The early years of the Grazing Service were euphemistically referred to as "clerks and cowboys," an era of loosely regulated land and mineral operations. In 1946 Congress established the Bureau of

Land Management, which merged the Grazing Service, General Land Office, and in western Oregon, the Oregon and California Revested Lands Administration, which represented railroad interests. At long last, at least from a management perspective, nearly two decades of relative calm ensued.

But by 1964, concurrent with the passage of the Wilderness Act, the general public's awareness of and interest in BLM lands had begun to change. Howard Zahniser, a member of the Wilderness Society who authored the act, underscored the changing perspective in his poetic definition of wilderness in the United States as land "in contrast with those areas where man and his own works dominate the landscape, is hereby recognized as an area where the earth and its community of life are untrammeled by man, where man himself is a visitor who does not remain." Based on that definition, 9.1 million acres of federal land were protected by the act. More practically, to be eligible for protection, proposed tracts had to be at least 5,000 acres, have little evidence of human impact, offer solitude, and possibly contain "ecological, geological, or other features of scientific, educational, scenic, or historical value." At approximately the same time, the BLM had begun looking at other uses for the lands that fell under its jurisdiction in view of all the new legislation or, in BLM parlance, began setting "multiple use management parameters."

No surprise . . . not everyone had the same vision for these acres. Some saw the public lands as refuge for plants and animals in need of protection. Some saw them as ideal for low-impact recreational use, such as hiking or mountain biking, while others defined recreation differently. Their gun scabbard mounted on their ATV, they headed for the desert hills. Newly minted off-road, all-terrain, go-anywhere vehicles showed up on public lands. Archaeological sites previously protected by their remote locations were suddenly being vandalized and looted. The BLM was originally tasked with assuming responsibility for lands in the West no one (government parlance for white settlers) wanted. Now everyone wanted them.

Unfortunately, just as the needs grew more urgent, the bureaucracy became more molasses-like. The BLM's ability to parse and police its turf became increasingly complicated with the passage of a flurry of acts and policies in the 1960s and '70s that resulted in months of negotiations about every darn thing. To wit: the passage of the National Environmental Policy Act in 1969 followed the Wilderness Act; the Endangered Species Act was passed in 1973; and 1976 saw the approval of the Federal Land and Policy Management Act declaring that BLM lands were "to serve present and future generations" and administer public lands "on the basis of multiple uses and sustained yield" of resources. How's that for open-ended? Lands that were mainly used for grazing as well as some timber and mineral harvest—a period from 1930 to 1960 during which the BLM focused primarily on extraction regulations, livestock numbers, and seasons of use—were now open for all kinds of conflicting businesses. In the West 248 million acres are currently under BLM management. In Oregon the agency manages 15.7 million, over a quarter of the state's land base. By now the BLM knows all too well it can't possibly envision what the demands on public lands might be in the future. It claims to be doing its level best to grapple with what is evolving, and I believe it is. To this day, the metaphorical BLM undercarriage is high-centered atop contradictory demands. Could the Oregon Desert Trail and the gentle interface it provides between different types of public land interests and users be what is needed to get the wheels of public lands management back on the ground?

The trail Fenty made real, inspired by the eight-hundred-mile Hayduke Trail of Utah and Arizona, provides a grand tour of the little-visited but jaw-dropping landscapes of eastern Oregon's high and dry. At 750 miles, the trail just scratches the surface of the largest desert in the United States: the cold, sparsely populated sage steppes of the 190,000-square-mile Great Basin Desert that stretches into Idaho, Nevada, California, and Utah. Oregon's trail may not be in the Hayduke's league, but it provides something increasingly hard to come by: respite from the hubbub of twenty-first-century life that the better-known national parks can no longer offer as they grapple with millions of visitors per year.

Fenty is quick to give credit to the hundreds of volunteers and the fifteen members of ONDA's staff who helped make the dream of this trail a reality, piecing together existing jeep tracks, overland routes, and trails through vast, dry stretches of predominantly public lands with occasional easements across private property. ONDA's former board member and GIS and map guru Craig Miller as well as the now-defunct Desert Trail Association that created a trail model replicated by the ODT were also key contributors to the effort.

There's so much to like about the Oregon Desert Trail, although, swallowed whole, it's not an easy trail to complete, and that's an understatement. Remote outposts, like Paisley, Frenchglen, Fields, and Rome (average populations one hundred), provide the only respite from long stretches without water or the chance to resupply. It is not an improved trail. No explanatory markers or outlooks with plaques explain Northern Paiute or early emigrant history, although there's plenty of both along the ODT. No information is posted about ranching, mining, or water distribution projects specific to the trail. No signs explain the rich geology the trail traverses or the flora and fauna you are likely to see. No campsites with picnic tables and outhouses. What there are, are maps, now online, and an exhaustive, highly informative trail guide kept up to date by ONDA's trail coordinator, Renee Patrick. Oh, and blog posts by thru-hikers are available on ONDA's website, which offers invaluable dos and don'ts for others planning to undertake the challenge. In a 2015 post by the trail's first autumn thru-hiker, Bob "Huck Finn" Jessee praised the trail's obscurity relative to other overused thru-hikes. "Perhaps the biggest highlight is the freedom I felt. The fact that the ODT is currently an idea more than anything else is awesome. I found any lack of structure/signage to be a positive. . . . No one can say, 'Well, that's not the trail,' or 'Huh . . . you're doing it wrong.' I love that it is a 'choose your own adventure.'"

Speaking of a thru-hiker's-eye view, let me introduce you to the first person to complete the entire route, Sage Clegg, who did so in 2013. Her intrepid spirit and savvy were evident in her charming and matter-of-fact instructional video about making a camp cook-stove out of a cat food can posted on her website. "People always say deserts are wasteland, but I don't see them that way at all. Deserts are filled with creatures who have a zest for life." Zest for life? She might as well have been describing herself. Once the trail was mapped via GPS, many hikers approached Fenty to be the first to thru-hike the full distance. For him, Clegg was the obvious choice. The trails she featured in her thru-hike résumé had inspired Fenty in the creation of the Oregon Desert Trail in the first place. She was more than qualified. Until 2018, when Heather Anderson of Washington completed all three in one year, Clegg held the women's speed record for completing the big three thru-hikes in the United States—the Appalachian Trail, Continental Divide Trail, and Pacific Crest Trail— knocking out that triple crown of roughly eight thousand miles and a million vertical feet of elevation gain in just under eighteen months. In 2011, she created a route across her home state of California, the twelve-hundred-mile Japhy Ryder Route from Death Valley to the Lost

Coast. A seasonal wildlife biologist specializing in tortoise research in Southern California's Mojave Desert, Clegg was no stranger to the quirks of desert terrain and temperature. Her main objective on the ODT was to maintain her already hard-core hiking chops but also, in concert with Fenty's objectives, to draw attention to one of the last great untouched areas of wildlands in the Lower 48. In Clegg, Fenty found someone who could "help us understand what we know and what we don't know," someone who understood the conservation value of a trail like this. She left the western terminus of the trail in the Oregon Badlands Wilderness east of Bend on June 11, 2013, and arrived at Lake Owyhee State Park on July 11 having hiked six hundred miles and biked the balance. As she stated to the *Bend Bulletin* after completing the trek: "I feel like hiking's usually kind of selfish. It was nice to know that maybe I'm helping create a trail for other people to come out and enjoy someday, too . . . bigger than myself." Since her thru-hike of the Oregon Desert Trail, an average of ten people per year have followed in her tracks.

Around the world, thru-hiking is a thing now. The young, the lean, and the restless travel the world in pursuit of bragging rights as they put another thru-hike notch in their belt, each trek equally or more challenging than the last. (If you can imagine it, by thru-hike standards the ODT is short, the average route being closer to two thousand miles.) Cheryl Strayed's book *Wild*, and the subsequent movie starring Reese Witherspoon, featured the author's experiences hiking the 2,650-mile Pacific Crest Trail. For the urban masses it popularized the idea of taking on a tough physical thru-hike as, in Strayed's case, a form of personal therapy as she recovered from the death of her mother, a divorce, and an appetite for recreational drugs. Shin splints, dehydrated dinners, and blisters became cool.

But hiking isn't only wasted on the young. It's big among the active over-fifty-five crowd seeking to explore the globe on two feet. In fact, retirees into their eighties have completed the ODT. Walking tours in Scotland as well as in the Nordic, Baltic, and Central European countries benefit from some version of England's and Wales's right-to-roam laws that permit access to private properties as the public enjoys trails embroidered over 3.4 million acres of hills, fields, moors, and downs.

Other options abound, from Nepal to Egypt, from the Temple Pilgrimage on the island of Shikoku in Japan, to walking any number of Camino de Santiago tributaries in France and Spain, to the most venerated of trails in the United States, the Appalachian Trail. It's actually a 2,181-mile daisy chain overseen by the National Park Service that links Shenandoah National Park in Virginia with lands managed by the Pennsylvania Game Commission, the Green Mountain Club in Vermont, the Appalachian Mountain Club in New Hampshire's White Mountains, and Baxter State Park in Maine. In concept or fact, thru-hikes in the United States and worldwide shaped Brent Fenty's vision for the Oregon Desert Trail.

Needless to say, I am no Sage Clegg. A self-proclaimed geezer jock who happens to love the high desert, I do what is more typical of the majority of ODT users: hundreds of us a year explore section by section, taking bite-size excursions where there is ready access, the landscape most scenic, returning to favorite ones, some stretches never attempted. Among the top ten on the ODT: Diablo Rim east of Summer Lake, Fremont and Abert Loop, Steens Mountain, Pueblo Mountains south of Steens, and most spectacular of all, the Pillars of Rome and West Little Owyhee Canyonlands in the far southeastern corner of Oregon. We're headed to these places. And always in our packs: water, food, compass, maps, matches, flashlight, bug repellent, sleeping bag—and the challenging questions to be answered as the demands on public lands intensify for a complex host of reasons as the need to build bridges between opposing points of view becomes critically important.

✦

Fenty cut his desert teeth growing up in Tumalo, a small central Oregon town perched on the edge of the high desert. He reflects fondly on the camping trips his family used to take. The out-of-doors immediately became the place he sought to feel part of something bigger, something mighty, wild, unblinking. His affection for the desert galvanized his commitment to the preservation of open and wild spaces, and it became his life's work. He prepared by getting an undergraduate degree in international studies and environmental science from Willamette University and a master's in environmental science from Alaska Pacific University. He then headed to ONDA, first as wildlands coordinator, then as executive director, and now as head of the relatively new Oregon Desert Land Trust, whereby private in-holdings are acquired to consolidate tracts of public lands and improve management. He knows about this. During his tenure as executive director, he worked on the implementation of the Steens Mountain Wilderness, a citizen's inventory of millions of acres of unprotected public lands, and campaigned successfully to designate the Oregon Badlands and Spring Basin as the state's newest desert wilderness areas. That was just a warm-up.

Seemingly tireless, both as ONDA's executive director and now in his new role, he thinks nothing of jetting to Washington, DC, to lobby legislators to forward land conservation proposals and to enact bills regarding land designations and permanent protection. Fenty follows in the footsteps of other Oregon land-use advocates and activists. Navigating the hallways of DC, he might well run into Andy Kerr, the man once considered the firebrand of the Oregon environmental movement. Thirty years ago, Kerr, with an assist from the endangered spotted owl, turned clear-cut logging into a national issue and himself into a figure deeply reviled by everyone and anyone working in the timber industry. As mill after mill shuttered due to the closure of federal forests, he attracted such headlines as "The Timber Industry's Most Hated Man in Oregon" (*Northwest Magazine*), "The Most Despised Environmentalist in Timber Country" (*Oregonian*), "Oregon's Version of the Anti-Christ" (*Lake County Examiner*). His response in a 2015 article in the *Oregonian* is vintage Kerr: "I had ten publicists working for me . . . not on my payroll, but on the payroll of the timber industry."

Kerr is now a Washington, DC, lobbyist and advisor to environmental groups. He has helped negotiate terms of legislation that created the Steens Mountain Wilderness in southeastern Oregon, one of the must-sees on the Oregon Desert Trail. He has worked on grazing buyouts and on the infamous Klamath Basin water wars. His judgments, according to the *Oregonian*, are "as arched as ever, his zeal to preserve wilderness undimmed." "I want it all," Kerr is quoted as saying about the Northwest's remaining wildlands.

After a few days of meetings, Fenty will fly back to central Oregon, leaving the bustle of DC behind. Jet lag is apparently not in his vocabulary. The next morning he'll think nothing of hopping in his pickup to drive long dirt miles to meet one-on-one with ranchers and still find time for family and for time alone in—guess where— the high desert. He seems wise beyond his forty-plus years. He has the affect of a track star—lean, strong, a drawn bow, loaded with energy and targeted purpose. As ONDA's executive director, Fenty took the organization farther than anyone could have imagined by engaging all concerned in thoughtful conversation, while doggedly pursuing efforts to legislate more wilderness. He embodies Adrienne Rich's sentiment:

> My heart is moved by all I cannot save:
> so much has been destroyed
>
> I have to cast my lot with those
> who age after age, perversely,
>
> with no extraordinary power,
> reconstitute the world.

Now, in his new role, the same level of accomplishment is anticipated.

When Fenty originally assumed the leadership of ONDA in 2008, the baton was passed to him by a larger-than-life barn burner, Bill Marlett, who became ONDA's first executive director in 1992. Considered by some to be on the radical end of the spectrum, Marlett became known for coining such slogans as "Cows Kill Salmon" as he campaigned to secure wilderness and make public lands cattle-free. "Collaborator" was probably not the word most associated with Marlett. Of sharp mind and wit, when I asked him about being a "radical," he replied, "I wish I were radical (i.e., having the ability to affect the fundamental nature of something), a work in progress." His motto: "The Golden Rule includes Mother Nature."

After graduating from the University of Wisconsin–Madison in 1977, Marlett worked for the Wisconsin Department of Natural

Resources protecting wetlands. In 1984 the City of Bend and Deschutes County hired him to help prevent hydro development on the Deschutes River, which morphed into his leadership of the Oregon Rivers Initiative to protect certain stretches of Oregon's special rivers as state scenic waterways. Senator Mark Hatfield upped the ante, according to Marlett, with the Oregon Omnibus Wild and Scenic Rivers Act. Both bills passed within a month of each other in 1988. Marlett then founded and, for four years, directed the Central Oregon Environmental Center in Bend before assuming the leadership of ONDA in 1993 for, he recalls, "a whopping monthly salary of $500." Under his direction ONDA grew as a force for wilderness preservation and livestock-free public lands. Marlett launched citizen-led wilderness inventories, convinced US Fish and Wildlife to remove livestock from Hart Mountain, persuaded the BLM to do the same along the Owyhee and Blitzen Rivers, and led the charge to create the first "cow-free" wilderness area in eastern Oregon on Steens Mountain. After nearly twenty years with ONDA, he remains a senior conservation advisor to the organization, although he has shifted much of his boots-on-the-ground environmental energy to the wildlands of the Baja Peninsula, working with local conservation groups to protect existing, and designate new, conservation lands.

Marlett's commitment to preservation and conservation started early, forged, he explains, the day he "came home from school to see a bulldozer ripping through the heart of Pheasant Branch Marsh [in Wisconsin]. . . . I was maybe thirteen at the time. The marsh was my playground and the beginning of my involvement in a community effort to create the Pheasant Branch Conservancy." Later, when he was in high school, his father gave him a copy of Aldo Leopold's *Sand County Almanac*. The following excerpt continues to motivate and inspire his every day.

We reached the old wolf in time to watch a fierce green fire dying in her eyes. I realized then, and have known ever since, that there was something new to me in those eyes—something known only to her and to the mountain. I was young then, and full of trigger-itch; I thought that because fewer wolves meant more deer, that no wolves would mean hunters' paradise. But after seeing the green fire die, I sensed that neither the wolf nor the mountain agreed with such a view.

Marlett has been motivated in his work by principle, yes, but also by the poetry of language, others' and, as evident in his quote that appeared in one of ONDA's early calendars, his own: "Wilderness is nothing more than a spiritual desire, if not a biological necessity, for people to be whole with their past, connected to a future; like the gates of a temple, the boundaries of wilderness are artificial, yet crossing that threshold allows feelings of a larger self, a nod of respect for what was, a sense of duty to what should be. Imagine a day when wilderness needs no boundaries."

✦

The birth of ONDA is the stuff of which "just do it" dreams are made. In 1985, eight years before Marlett took the helm, a classified ad was placed in the local Bend paper by one Alice Elshoff extending an invitation to anyone who cared about preserving the sagebrush steppe to gather and plan. The motley crew that showed up each threw in five dollars. Building on years of grassroots organizing and the high-desert wilderness inventory work by Don Tryon, a former Oregon Natural Resource Council staff member, the name Oregon Natural Desert Association was settled on and nonprofit bylaws drawn up.

You need to know Alice Elshoff. In the late '70s Alice and her husband, Cal, moved to the Malheur National Wildlife Refuge. The circumstances of the Elshoffs' move to the refuge underscores everything that Alice and her husband are known for: adventure, imagination, courage, can-do, and love of open spaces. As it happened, a two-hundred-acre ranch adjacent to the refuge that featured valuable water and habitat resources had been offered for sale but only if made part of the refuge. The owners and government representatives were stalled over price, so Elshoff and her husband not only loaned the extra amount to seal the deal but also signed on to live on the unoccupied ranch while working as volunteers on behalf of the refuge, pulling barbed wire fence, doing bird counts, and assisting visiting researchers. They overlapped Denzel and Nancy Ferguson, managers of the Malheur Field Station, an outpost of Quonset huts located near the refuge headquarters funded and operated at the time by a consortium of twenty-two colleges and universities for education and research. The Fergusons are best known for *Sacred Cows at the Public Trough*, their diatribe against cattle grazing on public lands. It included such slings and arrows as "No industry or human activity on earth has destroyed or altered more of nature than the livestock industry." Alice Elshoff wholeheartedly agrees, and this point of view has informed her high-desert conservation efforts. The Elshoffs remained at the refuge for the next decade. Lucky for the refuge, their love for the desert seemed to grow exponentially each year. Of her time at the edge of the Malheur refuge Alice recalls "the great spatial silence and the dark skies" or "joining the coyotes in appreciating a full moon." She currently serves as vice chair of the Friends of Malheur National Wildlife Refuge, incorporated as a nonprofit organization in 1999.

The ONDA of today—nationally recognized as a smart, informed, and effective nonprofit in the conservation movement—is a far cry from Alice summoning a handful of dedicated desert conservation advocates who shared her commitment "to make everyone in the country aware of how important our public lands are to everyone. Our public lands are the envy of the world, linking the past to the present. They have to be maintained and cherished." ONDA annually honors Alice's work, awarding the Alice Elshoff Desert Conservation Award to recognize individuals who make significant contributions to protecting Oregon's desert.

But Brent Fenty observes a more moderate approach, if not philosophy, than Alice Elshoff's, Bill Marlett's, the Fergusons', and certainly more than Andy Kerr's, an enfant terrible act hard to follow. Fenty worked diligently to win back the trust of ranchers post-Marlett who were still recovering from slogans such as "cattle free in '93" and who worried Fenty might be a wolf in sheep's clothing, that he too would just as soon see the cattle gone. In certain locations Fenty would, but he strived to accommodate ranchers' grazing needs in his sweeping public lands proposals while holding on to the support of his more hard-line ONDA constituents who believed cattle were the work of the devil. And he made no bones about his positions opposing extraction and energy interests. The differing perspectives on his board and within the ranks of supporters and naysayers kept him on his toes. He summed up the challenge this way: "From landowner to public land visitor, all want to protect a place they love. All are different manifestations of love. All define place and love differently." Make no mistake, however, he was and remains clear, very clear, about how he defines that love, and while he listens, he is always on the lookout for opportunities, fracture lines, ways to persuade.

Fenty has the DNA pedigree of Kerr and Marlett running in his veins along with the most powerful weapon of all, his passion and dedication "to protect, defend and restore" Oregon's high desert, the clarion call of ONDA.

There's good reason to do so. The eight-million-acre area in central and southeastern Oregon that ONDA makes its business includes the second-longest free-flowing river in the continental United States, flora and fauna particular to and requiring this landscape, and some of the most remote locations in America, including the largest swath of roadless area in the Lower 48 "that should but doesn't yet have federal protection," as Tim Neville wrote in the *New York Times* after a trip he took with Fenty into the Owyhee Canyonlands. Fenty hopes, ONDA hopes, that this desert will avoid being one more region where, as Fenty says, "man carries on his old habits, makes his old mistakes until the naturalness of the place is demolished." Without wildness, as the late David Brower of the Sierra Club said, the world is just that much closer to becoming a cage.

It has taken me a while to recognize that making lands accessible to the public serves to protect them. After two decades of ranching on a cow-calf operation that included twenty thousand deeded acres and eighty thousand acres of BLM land, I moved to town with my three children to navigate life as a single mother. Not only was I no longer a wife, but I was stripped of my adopted identity as rancher and landowner. Given that roughly 75 percent of the privately held land in the United States is owned by 5 percent of landholders, most of them white, it is an exclusive club. Ride or drive fifteen miles in any direction, this lily-white cowgirl was on land that my husband and I controlled. "Controlled." How's that for arrogance, ignorance? Nothing like "ownership," as ephemeral a concept as that is, to bolster a fragile sense of worth, self, home.

Now I found myself in a house on a street with garbage cans that were placed out on the sidewalk every Tuesday evening, where my young son could chat with the neighbor's daughter by stringing orange juice cans house to house. Gone was my sense of superiority, of big deal, of "owning it all" as author William Kittredge wrote in his book about growing up on a ranch in southeastern Oregon. It took a long time for me to embrace the notion of public land for all the public. I assumed the BLM allotments we benefited from on our ranch were a given, for the use of ranchers only. Because BLM privileges were generally bought and sold with ranches, they didn't seem "public" lands, rather "our" lands. I turned up my nose at public campsites, public trails, at joining the migration of humans into nature on overcrowded holidays.

My bad attitude could be traced to an early imprint. Growing up in white Anglo-Saxon Protestant New England, I was weaned on references to so-and-so's beach, dock, copse, tennis court. I was taught to eschew the public parks and recreational facilities. Those were for the townies, a.k.a. commoners, who lived year-round, God forbid, in what were colonized by the WASPs as summer communities. The children of summer folk were brought up to think they were better as defined by pedigree and net worth, even though, in my family's case, we'd barely hung on to a neglected sliver of private beach, couldn't afford the private beach clubs, and the old family house, built before the Civil War, was falling down around our ears. Shabby chic before shabby was chic. You'd have thought I would have flocked to public access. You'd have thought I would have pushed against the boundaries of private beaches and backwoods I wasn't allowed to freely access, would have sailed far out of Buzzards Bay, learned about wintering seals and herring migrations, but I dutifully stayed inside the lines of the culture's social dictates—sailing in Buzzards Bay in white-hulled Beetle Cats, taking tennis lessons wearing white shorts, shirt, and tennis socks with a mini snowball on each heel that kept them from slipping into the sneaker. I often reflected years later as I moved cattle on horseback out across greening meadows in the high desert, how lucky that my life led me to ranching. I was out-owning the owners. I was blazing my own trail. I was drawing way outside my native culture's lines. I was falling deeply in love with the desert.

But now here I was, a townie myself, living year-round on far less land than the old summer house claimed. And worse, I was relegated to the tight strictures of life in town, not painting on the big landowner canvas: calving, branding, haying, summer turn-out, fall gather; eagles, *my* eagles, circling on the wind, dust boiling up behind *my* pickup (never mind the bank's participation) as I drove the dirt miles to town. Our closest neighbor, fifteen miles away, was fond of telling us we were the gosh-darn best neighbors he'd ever had. We'd point out that we were his *only* neighbors.

The BLM field representatives were among many unannounced but welcome guests during those halcyon days of ranching. Iced tea. Shoot the shit. "Better ease up numbers of cattle on Camp Creek." Okay, we would. As was the policy, we shared fencing costs along the boundaries between deeded and BLM land, participated in creek-side rehabilitation efforts. Other than hunters in the fall, we seemingly were the only ones accessing BLM lands at the time, the only ones who wanted to.

But now, living landless in growing-like-crazy Bend, Oregon, three thousand miles removed from the cultural casinos where my frayed calling card might have some play, I look with horror at all the people, people, people escaping on weekends to the increasingly loved-to-death locations in and around Bend. The lakes in the Cascades are teeming with stand-up paddleboards, kayaks, and sailboats. In the Three Sisters Wilderness, access to South Sister, twenty-nine miles west of Bend, is soon to be regulated with a daily quota given that over three hundred have been recorded summiting the ten-thousand-foot peak on a single summer or fall day. The impact of loving this hike to death is all too visible on Google Earth where the trail has been worn as wide as forty feet in some sections. The overflow of people is inevitably squeezed out into the relatively overlooked high desert for outdoor enthusiasts of every ilk to get their open-space fix. I don't need to remind you that this is happening everywhere. As we proceed along the Oregon Desert Trail, it becomes the high-desert version of the canary in the coal mine: a dusky, beady-eyed wren with a disproportionately big song cautioning us all, everywhere.

Then I discovered ONDA. Though the organization for me raises as many questions as it answers, they are all good questions—important, bracing ones. Is a trail (or wilderness area) the imposition of a particular point of view? Is a designated wilderness a good thing, a natural thing, or as much of a disruption to a landscape as other uses? Is restricting or eliminating the harvest of grass, meat, and timber just pushing the problem on to other countries? Could the impact of conservation policies be an avoidance, a form of denial? William Cronon, author of the essay "The Trouble with Wilderness," cautions: "Idealizing a distant wilderness too often means not idealizing the environment in which we actually live, the landscape that for better or worse we call home." I am reminded of how it seems easier to help with, say, an orphanage in Africa than with poverty in our own cities. The challenge is to see dwindling wildness in our own backyards and go from there. Author and activist Charles Bowden, who died in 2014, put it more bluntly, as was his wont. "Environmentalism," he once said, "is an upper-middle-class, white movement aimed at absolution and preserving a lifestyle with a Volvo." In Bend that would be a Subaru or a Sprinter Van.

Notwithstanding these impossible questions, ONDA has afforded me a different way to engage with the desert, a different way to think about how the high desert is used. As a former rancher and a former New Englander, I now see that ownership must be redefined. How? Collaborative stewardship of open space. Owning caring, owning sharing, like a faith commitment, a commitment to something you can't touch in order to create something many can touch, can experience, so more people can come to know themselves by getting to know the big empty, where more can experience the rare moment Joseph Krutch describes: "Not when we see there is something worth looking at but the moment when we are capable of seeing." That is the goal. Not bragging rights. Not status. There are—have to be—solutions that work for all.

In May 2016, I stood in a long line behind Brent Fenty. We were waiting for a chance to shake hands with former president Bill Clinton, campaigning in Bend on behalf of his wife's presidential bid. Brent had taken his ten-year-old daughter out of school so she could also meet the former president. While we waited, Brent reminded his daughter of their family trip to Yellowstone National Park. The man she was about to meet was the one who signed legislation allowing for the reintroduction of wolves to that park. And the Grand Staircase–Escalante Monument? Did she remember going there? She nodded yes enthusiastically. The man she was about to meet created that national monument. From family dinner table conversations, Fenty's young daughter knew her father was working hard at the time to persuade Congress to set aside 2.5 million acres of wilderness as part of the Owyhee Canyonlands Conservation Proposal. Maybe one day she'd be able to go there and say to herself: "My father did that." But this day, she already had plenty of reason to be proud of her father's work, not the least of which was his role in getting the Oregon Badlands Wilderness approval across the finish line.

THREE

Bad to the Bone

FROM ONDA'S OFFICES in Bend, it is a twenty-mile drive to the Oregon Badlands Wilderness that Brent Fenty, in conceiving the Oregon Desert Trail, designated as the western access point and trailhead for the high-desert trek that leads all the way to the Owyhee Canyonlands.

When ONDA got serious about advocating for the creation of the Oregon Badlands Wilderness, the proposed area was a handful of privately held ranches with BLM permits attached. The idea had been circulating since 1980 when the BLM designated the Badlands as a wilderness study area. Given the players, ranchers versus government versus environmentalists, you'd think a standoff was the only possible outcome. But as it turned out, nothing in this part of the world brings strange bedfellows together like all-terrain vehicle operators who were regularly trespassing on the ranchers' land, scaring their cattle, cutting fences, and tearing up both the private and BLM ground. Ray Clarno, one of the ranchers with property adjacent to the proposed wilderness area, reputedly said giving up his BLM grazing allotment to have it designated roadless was better than dealing with four-wheelers. He had approached Bill Marlett in 1999 who managed to use wilderness legislation to facilitate land exchanges with the BLM and to close all the access roads to motorized vehicles. Prior to assuming the executive directorship, as an ONDA staff member Fenty reactivated and reenergized the effort in 2002, the year Oregon senator Ron Wyden introduced the first Badlands Wilderness bill in the Senate. The bill languished until 2008 when Fenty, in his first year as executive director, and Gena Goodman Campbell, ONDA's Badlands Wilderness coordinator, carried it across the finish line. ATVs were banned from the Badlands by the BLM. Four ranchers, all of whom owned adjacent land, retired their 2,971 acres of BLM cattle grazing allotments, adding them to the 26,000 acres of BLM land already secured. The successful collaboration was key in protecting and preserving the area and creating public access. The Oregon Badlands, now managed by BLM as a designated wilderness, enjoys the highest level of permanent protection.

This long, drawn-out conversation that started in 1980 ended as President Barack Obama's signature dried on the 2009 Omnibus Public Land Management Act. The creation of the Oregon Badlands offers a model of stick-to-itiveness and cooperation between government, conservationists, and landowners.

✦

Now only for the non-motorized public to enjoy, trekking through the Badlands can go one of two ways. You'll either develop a liking for the tough and chewy high-desert landscape that characterizes the entire Oregon Desert Trail, or if you don't, it's a safe bet you'll turn tail and run to greener climes. I like to think the Badlands have a face only a desert rat, as high-desert dwellers are known, could love—unwieldy, bristly, squint-eyed, ornery, and . . . volcanic.

Who among us knows what created the land beneath our feet, what hot moments, what excesses, what shrug of cold glacial shoulders? This forty-five-square-mile land-escape boasts mind-bending and time-warping features, starting with the powdery soil that coats your skin; it is dust largely from ash associated with the eruption of Mount Mazama seventy-seven hundred years ago. The trail takes hikers over subterranean lava tubes that provided special delivery systems for lava traveling thirty-five miles north to the Badlands from the Newberry Volcano that erupted seventy-five thousand years ago. The feverish excess of one flow popped a hole in the roof of the main tube, spewing hot rock that built the Oregon Badland's rootless shield volcano, a type composed almost entirely of fluid lava flows and, characteristic of the modesty of this desert, one that keeps a low profile, hence sometimes described as a warrior's shield lying on the ground. The irregularly shaped pit crater at the top of the shield marks the spot where lava oozed and drizzled in all directions to create the Badlands. A result of the hot-tempered history of the region is a cornucopia of beautiful rocks: obsidian, petrified wood, thunder eggs, and other brilliant constructs of molten magma.

Before moving to the high desert, I had never heard the term "rock hound." At the time it sounded distasteful somehow, something I didn't ever want to be, rather like a desert rat, both personae I now embrace. The waspy-est of WASPs taught me different. He had left Boston after college, taking his new bride to Ellensburg, Washington, to try ranching on for size. He ultimately succumbed to familial and cultural pressure and returned to Harvard Law School and a career at a fancy Boston firm. Once he reached his eighties, his idea of adventure had been reduced to his weekly ROMEO (retired old men eating out) meeting in downtown Boston. But as a middle-aged man his abiding love of the ranching West prompted him to visit our ranch more than once. "You lucky girl! You live in the rock-hound capital of the United States," he announced to me when I met him at the Redmond airport on the occasion of his first trip. "You know about rock hounds?" I asked incredulously. "Yes," he replied. "I am one."

I learned from him that I had unknowingly moved to a desert land of limb casts, moss agate, red and yellow jasper, and copper-colored sunstone—Oregon's gemstone, found north of Plush along the ODT. Compressed, crystallized, pulverized, scorched, shattered perfections birthed from volcanic upheaval and chaos millions of years ago, these stones worked their way to the surface, worked their way onto the smooth necks and soft earlobes of decorated women, onto the blunt ring fingers of men. I had moved to a state whose official rock was the thunder egg, to a place where people designed vacations around Petersen's Rock Garden, rock-hound festivals, Richardson's Rock Ranch, or the Spectrum Sunstone Mines, where people swerved off the road to stop and check out rock shops. One of my local favorites is designated by an enormous boulder nesting on the crushed roof of a garishly painted car in front of a straight-talking sign: "Rocks."

A rock hound is a hobby geologist, one who collects and studies rocks and minerals. And they do it in the most remote places, on their hands and knees, scratching, chipping, digging. They are armed with hammers, chisels, plastic bags, hand lenses, penknives, streak plates, magnets, and old dental tools. Rock-hound festivals are held throughout this part of the West, rock carnies tending collapsible aluminum tables laden with, well, rocks. Prineville's festival is held each June, followed by festivals in Redmond and Sisters. "Festival" suggests noise and gaiety. That's not the prevailing ambiance at a rock-hound festival or powwow, as they are commonly called, unless the clackety-clack of rock tumblers counts. More likely there's an assortment of RVs parked on the festival grounds and portable lawn chairs with coffee-toting beverage holders in the armrests set up alongside. There is a sense of time unlimited as people from all over the world meander through the maze of tables that strain under dusty wooden bins and Tupperware containers filled with what 90 percent of the population would never notice or remark on. But these rock hounds pick up and turn the stones and polished gems thought-fully, with respect and awe, look at them appreciatively, consider their violent history and the resolution of that journey into something they deem truly beautiful.

From what I have gleaned, the Great Basin region, the ODT country we'll be traveling, was twice submerged under water—first salt, unimaginably long ago, and then fresh. As the fresh water receded, when the Clarno volcanoes were active, exotic mammals—rhinoceroses, three-toed horses, strange camels, and boars—wandered the shores of lakes and feasted on lush vegetation. With the advent of the Pleistocene, ice inched its way down from Canada, damming the entire Columbia River. Steens Mountain boasted gla-ciers; Summer and Abert Lakes were part of one big body of water, an inland ocean. About this time the volcanic fireworks that formed the Cascades took the stage. Those peaks ultimately blocked precipi-tation, and the region that would become the high desert had to adapt to being a land of little rain with an annual average of nine inches.

Just as a thin ring of breathable air supports human life on earth, the habitable surface of the earth floats on a hot magma por-ridge only forty miles below. The basins of the great scarps of the high desert, such as Winter Ridge, Hart Mountain, Lake Abert, and Steens Mountain, all ODT highlights, are impressively close to the hot, molten stew of the earth's interior. Combine the hot air of that core with a freshwater source and the high-desert hot springs at these locations are the result.

Hot magma is always seeking a pathway to pitch a fit, boil up and through. The South Sister, with a growing bulge on its south flank, is currently contemplating just such a tantrum. But it is this dynamic and dramatic crucible of salt to fresh to volcanic crush to massive flows of ice that created the extraordinary fossil formations and exotic rocks that rock hounds find so compelling.

Initially, my rockhounding was—out of my newcomer's ignorance of the area's spectacular geology—limited to hunting for obsidian arrowheads in the spring. We had an Indian ranch hand who taught me where to look, what to look for. Our ranch was northeast of a well-known source of prized obsidian—Glass Butte, which erupted a mere 4.9 million years ago. It is south of the Oregon Badlands, easily visible from the ODT on the horizon to the south and east. So keen and in demand was this fire-glass for making arrowheads and knives, obsidian from this large land formation was found traded all the way to the Mississippi River and beyond. As Bendbased developer and high-desert rancher Bill Smith wryly observes, "Glass Butte is not given the pre-European credit it deserves. Glass Butte then was like Fort Knox is now: a pile of valuable material that made wealth."

The very words used to describe obsidian, which is formed by the rapid cooling of magma, sound hot and mysterious: chatoyant, iridescent, aventurescence. Fire, flame, and rainbow obsidian are all found on Glass Butte, as are the mahogany, gold, and sheen varieties. In the draws and coulees around our ranch, the runoff each spring would uncover fists of the black glass as well as chips and, in many cases, perfect arrow- and spearheads, and other tools. Some New Agers say obsidian protects, grounds, removes negativity while causing rapid change and learning. I didn't know that then, but in hindsight I'd have to agree. I feel both burnt and instructed, tumbled and protected by this desert.

When my youngest was four I was accepted into a writing workshop led by the author Ursula Le Guin. We would-be writers stayed in one of the old Quonset huts at the Malheur Field Station. We ate in the communal kitchen along with Elderhostel groups on birding expeditions and earnest graduate students studying the environs of landlocked Harney Lake. Ursula Le Guin, who died in 2018, was inspirational as a writer, an activist, a person. And she loved the high desert. During the workshop she shared that some of the fantastical landscapes in her writing were inspired by favorite places in and around Steens Mountain and the Malheur National Wildlife Refuge. In her wonderful, brave, imaginative, and mischievous way she seemed a cousin to the coyote. The vintage Ursula Le Guin slogan she came up with for the T-shirts commemorating our shared experience proclaimed: "Inveterate doer of this sort of thing."

As is typical of this sort of gathering of writers, we were a random group of people with little in common other than an interest in improving our craft. Or so we thought. It turned out that each of us had serendipitously stumbled on this opportunity to receive not only Le Guin's teachings but also those of this magical part of the world. Maybe those were obsidian chips on our morning cereal.

On one afternoon field trip we were taken to a nondescript location where there were said to be the thunder eggs we'd heard about, the "geode-like bodies with chalcedony or agate cores covered in layers of volcanic ash," according to the refuge pamphlet. One less-than-scientific explanation is that thunder eggs were made by surviving at least two volcanic eruptions, the second blast coating and cooking the solidified first—forming crystalline caverns inside the newly minted shell—often with loose particles of crystal that rattle when you shake the rock. The name *thunder egg* is said to derive from a Warm Springs Indian legend in which rival, jealous gods dwelling on Mount Hood and Mount Jefferson hurled thunderbolts at one another and the round-shaped thunder eggs were the result of these quarrels. We crawled around on the ground, picking up the brown spheres and shaking them vigorously next to our ears. I found three thunder eggs—or lava core bombs, as they are also called—one for each of my children, each with a different song sealed tightly inside.

For the participants in Le Guin's workshop the thunder egg was a fitting symbol. The retreat turned out to be the opportunity to honor being thunder-egged by our lives and taking the time to listen for, reflect on, and write about the fragile, glassy symphony that played inside us and those we loved.

Another rock encounter of the close kind occurred a few years later. I drove east with a friend out of Bend to walk along Dry River in the Oregon Badlands. The monumental rocks along this riverbed were smoothed by an ancient river that drained Lake Millican during a lull in the Ice Age. On the smooth faces of the boulders we saw urgent shaman-like figures with sun circles radiating from their heads, energetic deer figures, and cartwheeling stick figures. It was dusk when we left, the silhouettes of the gray-green juniper trees visible along the path. I happened to glance over at one as we passed, and there, cupped in the palm of a branch that extended toward me, was a crystal. No kidding. It was as though it grew there, the fruit of this tree. I accepted the gift, astounded by the mystery and magic of this happenstance.

In her book *Gathering Moss*, Robin Wall Kimmerer writes about suddenly being awakened to a world around her, one that had been there the whole time but not before apprehended. "A Cheyenne elder of my acquaintance once told me that the best way to find something is not to go looking for it. . . . He said to watch out of the corner of your eye, open to possibility, and what you seek will be revealed. The revelation of suddenly seeing what I was blind to only moments before is a sublime experience for me."

Now I pay close attention to the rock I carelessly wrap my rope around to secure my raft to the shore of the Deschutes River, the rock I use to hold down tent corners when camping in the desert, the rock I use to create a firepit, dislodge on an ascent up South Sister, skip across high mountain or desert lakes, rub on my heel to smooth calluses. I pay attention to the rocks that line my chimney or create the pockmarked wall between my neighbor and me or the ones I cast aside in irritation when gardening. Because I now know one might be offering a directional signal—or extending a hand in sympathy or support. And that includes the Riga mortised lava rock contortions, those ghouls and gargoyles of the desert that rear up along the ODT and yell "Boo!" They make the perfect dance partners for the sixteen-hundred-year-old twisted and contorted juniper trees that populate the Badlands.

Over the past decade, ranchers have taken to clearing younger juniper stands, often with the help of government grants, to restore groundwater, springs, and creeks. The young stands are considered invasive in the high desert due to their consumption of twenty to thirty gallons of water per day. Fires used to regulate their spread, but fire suppression practices have worked almost too well, the range of the tree increasing tenfold since 1930. Thankfully a pass is given to old-growth juniper, native to the badlands' volcanic soils. For these wizened trees, home sweet home is a little topsoil on top of Columbia River basalt. The ancient ones are easy to spot with their asymmetrical crown in lieu of a Dairy Queen swirl-shape sported by the young crowd. The bark of these old-timers is reddish with deep furrows, and their branches are often festooned with a garish green lichen, a kind of high-desert version of wisteria. In their presence you can't help but feel you're at the feet of an ancient and wise elder.

The Oregon Badlands (in fact the whole of the ODT and the high desert) is indeed an acquired taste, but once acquired you'll swoon for its irresistible beauty as it smooths your uneven edges in its rough and tumble. When you emerge from the crucible of the Oregon Desert Trail, you'll be polished, changed, lustrous.

Meandering through the land of "as good as it gets," be ready for bunchgrass, stands of big basin and Wyoming sagebrush, all heartbreakingly subtle in hue, pungent in fragrance. They join their reedy and small-leafed hands to embroider critical lekking areas for sage grouse and habitat for songbirds. The adaptation by flora and fauna to living in the high and dry is inspiring and instructive, such as the way sagebrush curls its leaves shut during the heat of the day to preserve the dew collected during summer nights. Sometimes a droplet of water can be seen, a shimmering bead cupped in this tiniest of palms.

After the snow melts, a riot of springtime wildflowers laughs away your blisters—such bright faces as balsamroot, long-rayed groundsel, Cusick's monkeyflowers, showy Townsendia, western wallflower, wild heliotrope, yarrow, milk vetch, and Oregon sunshine. Delicate white sand lilies bloom in early May, stately purple blue mariposa lilies proclaim July, and rangy yellow rabbitbrush is the hallmark of summer's end. Brilliant green lichen decorates rock faces; many of the lichens coveted for dyes by those who card their own wool.

In addition to the unique flora of the high and dry, all kinds of wildlife inhabit the Badlands and will populate your Oregon Desert Trail safari. Yellow-bellied marmots (also ignominiously referred to as rock chucks or whistle pigs), porcupines, elk, coyotes, deer, bobcats, rabbits, black bears, mountain sheep, burrowing owls . . . and that's just for starters. The vast open is perfect for pronghorns to show off as the second-fastest land mammal in the world after the cheetah. This distant cousin to the giraffoid got so speedy over the slow course of millions of years of evolutionary practice running away from a Pleistocene cheetah-like predator that, back then, also called the high desert home. Another high-desert staple is the Townsend ground squirrel, or sage rat as they are referred to locally. They charmed my mother when she visited from the East Coast. She referred to them as exclamation points running across the road, tails straight up in the air. Central Oregon farmers and ranchers have a very different opinion, their fields pocked with sage rat holes and mounds, treacherous for horses and hell on irrigation systems. Every spring, hunters from town would stop at our ranch to get permission to come on our property and tune up their marksmanship on the varmints scurrying across the fields. I'd let them so long as they brought me the dead rats. Handing over their catch, they'd watch in horror as I slipped the hapless creatures into Ziploc bags and dropped them into the freezer chest in the boot room of the ranch house. The hunters hurried away, jumping into their trucks and gunning it, no doubt persuaded the years of living out had gotten to me, that sage rat was a delicacy on my family's menu. In fact, I took the frozen ground squirrels to the High Desert Museum, located near Bend, to feed wounded raptors. Along the ODT you'll glory in the variety of the birds of prey that thrive in the wild, the lucky ones who have avoided power lines, windshields, and rehabilitation at the museum. Ospreys, red-tailed hawks, bald and golden eagles glide on the updrafts. Owls will call to you at night. With nothing but time, sinister turkey vultures circle lazily, hoping you'll lose your way.

In anticipation of a thru-hike or, alternatively, hiking short sections of the ODT, a visit to the High Desert Museum is a must. This national treasure offers short and long courses on the natural, social, and cultural history of the high desert through exhibits and engaging programs. You can time-travel sitting at a kitchen table inside an authentic homestead or visiting a small sawmill. You can learn about the rich and storied Northern Paiute and Columbia River tribes' cultures in the high desert, past and present. By way of preview, the museum offers close-up views of the wildlife that call the ODT home: river otters, bobcat, osprey, and eagle. High desert amphibians, lounging in fancy desertariums, are on display, including the spotted frog that has been making endangered species headlines, and the always-mesmerizing reptiles—lizards and snakes. Just try and win a stare down with the (literally) unblinking gaze of the bull snake or Great Basin rattler that, in the wild, favor the Badlands' flat, sunbaked rocks in the cool of the evening.

By the way, don't cancel a trek through the high desert because you're afraid of snakes. They are far more afraid of you. If you think you're in snake territory, clap, make noise, let them know you're coming. They aren't big on surprises. Thru-hiker Mary "Fireweed" Kwart suggests carrying hiking poles "to make snake encounters less likely in tall grass." Most who live in the desert respect the rattlesnake and leave it alone, unless and until it is too close to home. A cowboy acquaintance of mine mastered the questionable practice of sneaking up on a rattlesnake that favored the sunny back stoop of his ranch house by grabbing its tail and whiplashing it with such force, the neck of the snake snapped. My own anecdote that gave new meaning to "a snake in the grass" was when my firstborn, six months old at the time, was playing contentedly on a blanket on the lawn behind our ranch house. I was gardening nearby, and between us, a lawn sprinkler. I assumed the hissing I heard was a leak in the sprinkler hose. But it wasn't. It was a Great Basin rattlesnake coiled, ready to strike my infant daughter. Don't ask me how, likely with the garden hoe, but that snake was instantly chopped into pieces. It was the first time I personally experienced the instinctive, involuntary response of a mother protecting her young. Rattlesnake stories abound, but in truth the average number of bites in Oregon annually is around fifty, nationally only seven thousand, and they rarely cause death. On the off chance you do get "snake bit," do not apply a tourniquet, remove jewelry in anticipation of swelling, and find a doctor.

The real culprits on the ODT are much smaller and less fabled: mosquitos and ticks. West Nile virus and Saint Louis encephalitis, which usually present as flu-like diseases, are spread by mosquito bites and have been found in the counties along the ODT. Standing water and warm temperatures are mosquitos' idea of heaven. In the spring and summer if you see the Marlboro Man with his white tube socks pulled ingloriously up over his Wrangler pant cuffs, take note. Central Oregon's wood and dog ticks, carried by deer and hanging out on sagebrush and other low-growing shrubs, not only carry Rocky Mountain fever but now, with the arrival of the Ixodes tick, Lyme disease. Named after the small town of Lyme in western Connecticut where it originated, it has now migrated to the high desert, which is testament to the fact that, in good ways and bad, we are one, citizens of a borderless planet earth. The infections from Lyme disease and Rocky Mountain fever cause a wide variety of symptoms that sound like the warnings issued on television for nearly every drug advertised: fever, joint aches, fatigue, facial palsy, neck stiffness, rapid heart rate. Perhaps the one symptom tick-borne diseases do not claim is an erection lasting over four hours.

If you're out in the desert it is recommended to check yourself each night for ticks during the summer months. If you're on a long hike, check yourself in the morning and shake out bedding and previously worn clothing, just to be sure. If you find a tick attached to your body, don't panic. Even if the tick is carrying Lyme disease, it takes twenty-four to forty-eight hours for it to introduce the bacterium responsible for the disease into the bloodstream. Grasp the tick with tweezers close to where it's attached to the skin, and pull it out gradually without twisting. Put the removed tick in a plastic bag or a small container. If you develop a bull's-eye-like rash, a telltale sign of having contracted Lyme disease, hightail it to a doctor. Along the ODT there are medical clinics at Christmas Valley, Lakeview, and in other towns near the trail.

Snakes, ticks, lizards, and vultures, grit and grime, rough and rugged terrain populated by spooks of sharp rock. No wonder this wilderness area is called "badlands." Actually, many places are: Grand Staircase–Escalante National Monument in Utah, Badlands National Park of South Dakota, Toadstool Geologic Park in northwestern Nebraska, El Malpais National Monument in western New Mexico. There are others in Canada, New Zealand, and Europe. What they all have in geologic common is thin skin. Regolith. It is the Greek term for "blanket rock," unconsolidated rock and dust that sit atop a layer of bedrock. Like a loosely woven summer blanket. Thin skin over bedrock. Despite what masks as toughness, the high desert is thin skinned, literally and figuratively, and calls for a light touch and tread.

✦

I don't know about you, but I am struck by how we're uncannily led to the places that will teach us what we need to learn: peripheral vision, alertness to pattern, to trend, to infinitesimal shift—socially, scientifically, visually, ecologically, and personally. It's the sequence of the places we live that makes up the chapters in our biography of place. The high desert is, without question, my longest chapter. Where does my biography of place begin? I'd have to say among deciduous trees, brambles, fireflies, and smooth granite rocks found along the shores of Lake Cochichewick or else among the kelp and sea glass and shells on the shore of Buzzards Bay in Massachusetts. It includes lying on my stomach in my snowsuit as a child, contemplating what seemed another planet when looking down through the black ice of Rhode Island's Big and Little Wash Ponds; on the Fourth of July, leaping into Potter Salt Pond to retrieve tennis balls shot from an old cannon by our eccentric neighbor; following the potato harvester with my mother, collecting baby potatoes the tines of the harvester missed. It would be much later I learned that those ponds, the acres of dense woods surrounding them, the potato fields that ran to the Atlantic Ocean, were privately owned. Like so much in New England, they were part of the property of generations-old New England families. The few households that bordered their land were allowed access. That included my family. The paths through the woods and fields were maintained by the property owners, but to me, as a child, those places didn't belong to anyone, they belonged to everyone.

My biography of place goes on to include swings through far-flung continents during my twenties, including in Africa, first with the Peace Corps and later as a graduate student. I then landed, as a bride gone West, in eastern Montana's Yellowstone County, where I recaptured the rough and smooth, the pearl-and-oyster lifestyle I had experienced and loved in Africa, later repeating it in the far reaches of Crook, Deschutes, and Lake Counties of central and southeastern Oregon and in high-desert places like Long Hollow, Twelve Mile Flat, Sanford Creek, Logan Butte, Punchbowl. My ranching years in Oregon trace the Crooked River, having lived and ranched on the South Fork and the upper and lower Crooked River. These locations and the points in between speak of places and relationships that add up to me, a me by now as gnarled and storied as an ancient Badlands juniper tree. Had it not been for harbors, woods, and ponds as a child, I wouldn't know the vocabulary of stillness, contemplation, observation, or the willingness to fall head over heels for something I couldn't name. I wouldn't have learned to look for the real and metaphorical understory in the forest or find the "riverteeth," as author David James Duncan describes: "the hard, cross-grained whorls of human experience that remain after all else has been washed away."

My first experience of the ranching West was a summer spent in Birney, Montana. I returned East to my first year of college in the urban noise and haste of Boston and tried to write a poem about the impact of seeing, for the first time, that kind of abundance of open space, plumes of dust boiling up behind a pickup disappearing over the horizon on a dirt road, red canyon walls, cavvies of horses running, running, the self-sufficiency of the existence. I've mercifully lost the poem, a naïve promise to live in the rural West, but I remember one line: "I'll take my water from the ground up, thanks." The poem did not resonate philosophically or creatively with my professor, the poet Robert Fitzgerald, who was perfectly happy to live right where he was in Cambridge, Massachusetts. But for me the desire for a simplified, more direct, more real relationship with people and the land was precipitated by that experience in the tiny community of Birney on the Bones Brothers Ranch. It was written.

In constructing your biography of place, notice how many locations are now or, perhaps, always were man-handled, -shaped, and -made; spaces you move through in predetermined fashion according to architectural renderings. Strolling through the farmers' markets set up in brand-new, shiny, beautifully articulated neighborhoods, with live-work, big and small, cheek-by-jowl and larger lots, the just-right sprinkling of shops—your passage, your movement orchestrated by a tamed place. What wild places have you experienced? Yours to freely explore? And what do you imagine your children and grandchildren will include in their biographies of place? The pre-fab neighborhood, the mall (or *mal* as my father aptly called them, French for "bad"), a carefully manicured golf course or ski slope? When my children were young, and the sport was new, some parents' cars sported bumper stickers proclaiming: "Skateboarding is not a crime." In Bend the advent of snowboarding was greeted with the same suspicion. A sport that grew from skateboarding, a sport designed by the young, for the young, without adult supervision can't be good. Ski schools were late to the party, looking with disdain at what would soon take over the slopes, belatedly offering lessons in their renamed "snow sport" schools embarrassingly long after it had taken hold among all age groups. It's well documented how legislated the time of young people is, and generally in one activity after another in which an adult is telling them how to do it "right."

Lifelong learning at any age requires silence, daydreaming, sitting in the sun observing an ant hill or a spider making a web, without being called to get in the car to go to soccer or tennis or ballet or math tutoring. The dwindling number of us with firsthand experience with, or a penchant for, the organized chaos of nature, of wildness, directly parallels the loss of wilderness, not because we're loving it to death, but because our habits as a society and lack of understanding of the impact of those habits is killing the wildness, is killing the Brownian movement, the messiness, the unpredictability, the drop-dead magnificence of nature. And as the distance between us and nature grows, the less we care and notice about the natural world, including one another. Author, poet, naturalist, raconteur, philosopher, and wonder man Robert Michael Pyle notably wrote: "People who care, conserve; people who don't know, don't care. What is the extinction of the condor to a child who has never known the wren?"

A relatively recent entry into my biography of place is the Deschutes River. I now live on its banks. In the 1990s the City of Bend seemingly randomly decided it was no longer a crime to swim in the Deschutes River as it flows through town, stopped giving young people fines for jumping in, and lifted all bans from using the river recreationally. Maybe the police couldn't keep up, maybe the Chamber of Commerce whispered into the City's ear. Now, in addition to there being a waterpark upstream from my house, including an artificial wave for surfers and kayakers that costs taxpayers plenty, the river is jam-packed with people floating by in inner tubes, astride grotesque pink flamingos, or luxuriating in the equivalent of an inflated lounge complete with mug holders and back rests. Does it bother me? The noise and commotion? Boom boxes? F-bombs? Trash discarded into the river? The trumpeter swans are gone. So too the invasive mute swans. Otters are scarce; you almost never see them happily floating by on their backs munching on a crawfish, another population that has also diminished in the section of the Deschutes River that flows through Bend. I don't know the health of iconic river insects that fly fishermen rave about: caddis, may, stone, midge.

There is, however, a new hatch in town that has their attention. A fly-fishing houseguest of mine chortled appreciatively, watching the scantily clad females float by, "Good bikini hatch this year!"

Having said, a beaver removed three of my trees last spring, raccoons have figured out how to slide open my screen door, and deer take refuge in my urban yard. I think the wildlife is okay-ish with the floaters . . . for now. I posit that some of those going by with beer and chips and waistlines that suggest the need for more exercise don't often do this sort of thing. Sometimes, as the adults drift noisily past my house, often punctuating every sentence with a profanity, I notice their children, oblivious to their parents' rowdiness, fall into a dreamy and reverential silence, one hand dragging in the water. They feel the pull of current, smell the dank river, speculate about things just beneath the surface. That float trip becomes a short but important entry into their biography of place. So, no, I am not bothered by the noise and commotion. To be sufficiently moved to save a place (well, anything), you have to love it, and to love it, you have to talk to it, get up-close and personal with it. The press of humanity eating at the edges of government lands and pressuring private landowners are these people, *we* are these people. There is no *them*, only *us* in this. To the extent we develop an understanding of what the river says and wants, we will work together to protect it.

And these families on the river are outdoors! That alone is noteworthy in comparison to the national statistic that we're spending 93 percent of our time indoors. In many parts of America and the world, it's telling and troubling that people have to be guided through the forest and taught how to appreciate it. Increasingly more and more books are written about getting out and enjoying nature phone-free. The remedies being offered only reveal how removed from the world of the out-of-doors we have become. In Japan, a popular trend is called forest bathing, *shinrin-yoku. Shinrin* means "forest," *yoku* means "bath." Dr. Qing Li, in his book *Forest Bathing,* offers basic instructions. That we need them is the horror. "First, find a spot. Make sure you have left your phone and camera behind." He continues, "After guided walking aimlessly, drink in the flavor of the forest and release your sense of joy and calm. This is your sixth sense, a state of mind. Now you have connected with nature. You have crossed the bridge to happiness."

There is an oxymoron in this quote. I wish it were funny, but it further underscores how out of touch we are with the natural world: "After guided walking aimlessly." Guided and aimless at once. How exactly does that work?

A friend of mine described trailing a father and his young daughter up Black Butte, a popular hike in central Oregon. The youngster was complaining every step of the way, according to my friend, begging to go back to the nearby resort of Black Butte to watch television, be reunited with her video games. "We're in the woods," said the father. "Look how pretty. Wait until you see the view from the top. We're in nature!" His daughter replied, "But I already watched two *National Geographic Kids* yesterday! Isn't that enough?" Author Peter Forbes feels the fact that children are not in nature is a call to arms, a motion seconded by the author of *Last Child in the Woods,* Richard Louv. But how to do this? David Sobel of the Center for Place-Based Education points out that all too often "between the end of morning recess and the beginning of lunch, schoolchildren will learn that ten thousand acres of rainforest will be cut down. Then they'll be told that by recycling their *Weekly Readers* and milk cartons they can help save the planet." But if they don't know about the mysteries contained in the meadow behind their school, are they likely to try? The problems they hear about are too big, too faraway. Too much bad news. Some shut down. Avoid eye contact with nature. PTSD of the save-the-planet kind. They want to hang out where the electrical outlets are, not where a bullfrog lives. Other young people, however, offer a compelling alternative to withdrawing. Like the young plaintiffs in Eugene, Oregon, who sued the federal government for insufficient action on climate change or the intrepid Swedish teenager Greta Thunberg, nominated in 2019 for the Nobel Peace Prize for her environmental activism. By creating and recording our biographies of natural places, past and present, maybe we can chart a geography of legitimate hope for the future, for ourselves and our children.

We can now add the Badlands of central Oregon to our biography of place! It only gets better from here. Making our way south and slightly west, we reach Dry River, where I was gifted the crystal and which marks the southeast boundary between the Oregon Badlands and Horse Ridge, two distinct volcanic areas. The abundance of water that churned through the canyon during several ice ages is only a memory for the deep, dry slot canyon. Inscribed on its walls, other memories: renderings of First Peoples' rituals, hunting scenes, mysterious geometric patterns, depicting Native biographies of place, stunning in their simplicity, noisy in their silence. Created as early as seven thousand years ago until as recently as the late 1800s, both pictographs (drawings or paintings) and petroglyphs (carvings) are common to canyons along the Oregon Desert Trail. James Keyser, in *Indian Rock Art of the Columbia Plateau*, explained that much Great Basin rock art was made by shamans acquiring or using supernatural power possibly during a trance. Others were likely illustrating the seasonal rounds and rituals of these high-desert hunter-gatherers. And some may illustrate the ribald Native American sense of humor, may be the equivalent of carving a heart and initials in a tree, as I speculate in this excerpt from my poem "Picto-Prayers":

But who is to say these pictos
aren't just billboards? Good hunting
and fishing ahead! Wild onions!
Or maybe Native graffiti inscribed
just after passion's consummation?
Little Fawn and Rides-the-Wind
did it here, a moon phase indicating
date, pierced circle—the hot-
blooded action.

The Badlands had fun with the molten lava mainlined from the Newberry Volcano, shaping lava sandcastles and flamboyant formations. The vast landscape informed the wall art, as it did Native American and white settler myths and stories, a means of making sense of the wild land they lived in.

Oregon poet and author Jarold Ramsey dedicates a section to Paiute stories in his book *Coyote Was Going There: Indian Literature of the Oregon Country*. He illustrates how their plain song mimics the mystical inscrutability of the petroglyphs, how their tales underscore the notion that laughter is the best medicine when trying to make sense out of what makes none. The nomadic and resourceful Northern Paiutes moved in small bands across the high desert, the groups identified by the foods they harvested in the territory they traveled. The Oregon Desert Trail traverses the Paiute routes of the Pine Nut

Eaters (Paisley), the Berry Eaters (east of Steens Mountain), and the Wada (seed) Eaters (Malheur Lake). In *Coyote Was Going There*, Ramsey writes,

> The Paiutes' world was and is bleak, open, inhumanely spacious . . . and their stories evoke this great emptiness unforgettably—a blank space, with here a sagebrush, there a rock (both capable of talking), and over on the horizon, a butte. Time is a spring that has gone dry. Then someone appears, traveling through, Coyote perhaps. And he happens to meet another wanderer, and . . . these Paiute stories seen to be premised on the fact of sheer desert space— the ecological imagination in them seems somehow wilder, more manic than in other (tribes') repertories, as if driven to fill up endless and nearly featureless vistas with outrageous characters and explosive events.

Here is one of the stories from Ramsey's book:

HOW THE ANIMALS FOUND THEIR PLACES

In the old time, Coyote was boss.
Coyote said, "Bear, you better stay in the mountains."
Deer said, "I want to go live in the mountains too!"
Sucker said, "I want some water."
Duck said he wanted water too.
Swan said, "Look at me, I am growing pretty now;
See, I am white all over."
Bear pounded the ground.
"Ground," he said, "who is still talking about me?"
Ground said, "Indian talks pretty mean,"
So Bear went out and bit him.

"I want to stay here in the rocks,"
Said Mountain Sheep.
"I like to feel the ground," Rock said,
"I like to stay here in one place and not move."
Sagebrush said he felt the same way.
This is Coyote's story.

For more, Ramsey considers Wilson Wewa's collection *Legends of the Northern Paiute* required reading. The book is, Ramsey points out, "the first presentation of Paiute oral tradition by a tribal member. His tellings represent a real breakthrough, not just because they come from 'inside' (mainly from his grandmother, Maggie Wewa) but because he has worked out a way of transcribing them so that reading them is like hearing them!" Wewa's book tells stories about well-known central Oregon natural features, such as Smith Rock State Park, now a popular rock-climbing destination and the home of the 350-foot spire commonly known as Monkey Face. According to Wewa, however, the towering formation with its huge rock mouth agape, was called "Swallowing Monster" by his ancestors. Ask any climber who has attempted the sheer basalt tower and they would likely agree.

White settlers also tried to make sense of where in God's high desert they had landed, relying on a good sense of humor to help explain what couldn't be explained. They invented such roadrunner-like mythical creatures as the jackalope, a fearsome jackrabbit with antelope horns. The word is a portmanteau of *jackrabbit* and *antelope*, although the jackrabbit is a hare, not a rabbit, and the pronghorn is not an antelope. Calamity? Blame it on the jackalope! The unrelenting wind was likewise the main character in many desert tales. In *The Oregon Desert*, Reub Long tells about "one wind that blew a sage hen against a rock cliff and held her there until she laid eleven eggs. Easter occurred during this time and two were Easter eggs." The reader board in front of the Summer Lake store reads: "Wind? What wind?" Ranchers and cowboys in the desert can be tricksters to rival Coyote in Native American lore. A rancher I knew loved to fill the neighboring rancher's rain gauge after a light rain. Fooled time and again, the neighbor came hell-bent in his pickup to report the astounding number of inches that miraculously fell on his ranch only.

From regolith to myth, jokester to mystic, the high desert has it all. And we've only just begun this high-desert safari. Hold on to your hats as we leave the Oregon Badlands, trudge down Horse Ridge, and strike out across a sagebrush flat toward Pine Mountain.

FOUR

A Mountain Is
Pretty Sure to Figure

ONE OF THE "highs" along the Oregon Desert Trail, at sixty-three hundred feet, is Pine Mountain, located thirty-four miles southeast of Bend this side of the small community of Brothers. After cresting Horse Ridge it comes into view. Though there are many more dramatic and breathtaking mountains to enthrall day-trippers and thru-hikers on the ODT, this is the only one with an observatory perched on its flank, proffering the enticing invitation to look up.

Owned and operated since 1967 by the University of Oregon's Physics Department, the Pine Mountain Observatory (PMO) is open to the public for stargazing business on weekends from the end of May through mid-September. The cost of admission has most definitely not kept pace with inflation, a suggested five-dollar donation. Add to that a Forest Service campground adjacent to the observatory, and it's worth an overnight stay while on the ODT. The mission of the observatory is evenly split between research on white dwarf stars, the examination of large-scale galaxies, and a commitment to public education. High school groups come on field trips and are supported by the PMO in the analysis of the data they collect and the preparation of related papers. Night sky guides (observatory staff) are available to answer questions. Pine Mountain Observatory has also created software for K–12 teachers to perform observations and draw stellar conclusions from the comfort and convenience of their classrooms. Housed under UFO-like silver domes, the observatory has three different Cassegrain reflectors as well as a fourteen-inch telescope installed in 2015 that is operated remotely from the University of Oregon campus for research by undergraduate students.

For the Pine Mountain Observatory staff, looking up is their profession—punching the time clock at dusk and heading for bed at dawn. For amateur astronomers, it is a passion. The need they have in common is a pitch-black night sky.

As a young boy at a badly needed appointment with an optometrist, the dedicated amateur astronomer Richard Berry remembers he could hardly see the largest *E* on the eye chart. Then he got glasses. He describes it as going from "the letter to the infinite." He turned his gaze to the stars and has remained fixed on them ever since. Telescopes inside small shedlike structures populate his llama pasture on his Stayton, Oregon, farm. "From my observatory, I can capture images of everything from comets, like Comet 46/P Wirtanen now passing close to the Earth, to asteroids—such as my namesake, 3684, Berry—as well as nebulae, star clusters, and distant clusters of galaxies halfway across the universe." Berry is considered one of the foremost astronomers working in astrography, according to Dr. Alton Luken of the Pine Mountain Observatory. Berry works with a super-sensitive digital camera attached to a special telescope called an astrograph and has run exposures of twelve thousand seconds "catching faint clouds of interstellar dust," as he describes it.

But his farm on the western slopes of the Cascades is not the sanctuary for darkness it once was. "Light pollution is a big problem for anyone making images of celestial objects," Berry says. "From here is Lyons—just a tiny town—but lights from the Freres lumber mill smear light all over the southern sky. Salem creates a light dome that is worst to my west, but even the overhead and eastern night skies are much brighter than any natural sky. And Portland, even though it is some seventy miles distant, glows on the northern horizon." His solution? "From time to time, I take a small telescope to the east, to the high desert where the light of the cities is finally reduced to smudgy discolorations on the western horizon."

Encroaching light pollution on observatories located near larger cities makes Pine Mountain all the more important. But even PMO is noticing changes. In direct proportion to Bend, Redmond, and Prineville's growth, the darkness north of the observatory is increasingly compromised, not unlike the pressure being felt on other types of wilderness in central Oregon due to the exponential population increases in the area. The light domes over Bend, Redmond, and Prineville are broadening. When your day begins at dark, your research and livelihood dependent on pure darkness, this matters. Dr. Luken, who minds the astrological store at Pine Mountain, admits he is a sky crusader, "hopelessly impassioned" about what he does. Looking into the future, he anticipates Bend and Redmond will eventually merge into a single light dome. When that happens, Luken predicts the negative impact will be significant. As it is, there are already "signs of compromise," he says. Circumpolar constellations, like the Big Dipper, to the northwest of Pine Mountain are getting harder to see even above the thirty-degree mark. Generally speaking, astronomers don't concern themselves with stars below thirty degrees, zenith (straight up) being ninety degrees. The reason? The air mass gets thicker the lower on the horizon you go. Says Luken, "We don't flirt with the low regions. Too much air in the way."

But, Luken reassures, if the observatory had to choose where to locate itself for consistent views of the Milky Way, Pine Mountain remains as good a spot as any, given that the center of the cross-section of the Milky Way runs east and west over Pine Mountain and will never migrate toward the light domes. He is quick to remind, we are not looking *at* the Milky Way but out through it. We are in and of it. Dr. William Kowalik, an associate of Luken's, sent me a show-stopping image taken at the Pine Mountain Observatory of the Milky Way rising to the east, where the skies are still dark despite the man-made light interference to the west. Fiery. Braided. Dragon-like. Ferociously beautiful, powerful, humbling, magnificent. Jack's Beanstalk snaking up and over the night sky. That it's hard to wrap our heads around the notion we're looking from the inside calls attention to our tendency to see everything as other—peoples of different colors, cultures, religions—or taking place elsewhere—drought, flood, famine. Cartoonist Walt Kelly's twist on Commodore Oliver Hazard Perry's words comes to mind, "We have met the enemy and he is us."

With all the talk of light, moving toward light, light and life, you light up my life—the loss of darkness, the loss of the obsidian pitch blackness, of the raven abyss might seem a good thing. Darkness is associated with something foreboding, evil, undesirable, and in the case of outer space, an unfathomable infinity, a stark reminder of the human race's small purchase on things. So go ahead, look away. Look at something you know, like yourself.

But how about when we can no longer see the glowing mantle of stars overhead? When there is no backdrop for the heavens' excesses and infinities? We'd be doomed to a world dominated by artificial light, metaphor intended. The world as bright as Times Square. Endless illuminated reflections of ourselves projected back at us, underscoring our lack of self-reflection. Our imaginations would be stunted thanks to our obscured view of and relationship with the Milky Way, the inspiration for speculation, exploration, and limitless dimension, and our home, after all. The stars—including our sun that teeters on the edge of this spiral fanfare of clusters, chains, and ribbons—that also call this galaxy home, have beckoned us, confounded us, mapped our passage since time began. We'd be lost without them. According to a common medieval legend, when walking the Camino de Santiago pilgrims believed that the Milky Way, always overhead as they made their east-to-west journey across Spain, was created by dust kicked up by their feet. Perhaps hikers on the ODT will adopt this belief, will kick up a new Milky Way or, at least, commit to protecting the one we have.

Whether humans are a passing fancy or destined for a longer stay on the planet, you can't say we lack for ingenuity and, when applied to the good of all, the ability to inspire. Take Roger Worthington, who jumped on Bend's brewery bandwagon in 2013 (now over twenty craft breweries are in the town and at least thirty in central Oregon) and then went one big step further. Offsetting (or complementing) his entrepreneurial ambitions, he mixed into his craft brews his philosophies and hopes for the planet, literally. Adjacent to Worthington's nearly thirty-four-thousand-square-foot brewery is an organic hops garden where Oregon State University students can practice the craft brew trade. Not only does Worthy Brewing offer a series of lectures put on by the Oregon Natural Desert Association, but he built an observatory—make that an Hopservatory—for the public on the top of his building.

Since 2014 the administration of the Hopservatory has been in the capable hands of an avid amateur astronomer, Grant Tandy. He runs solar viewing and nightly viewing programs, greets school groups, and collaborates with other regional observatories to encourage awareness and curiosity about the galaxy we call home. With Pine Mountain Observatory, Worthy Brewing is one in a trifecta of observatories in central Oregon, the third being Sunriver's Oregon Observatory, which impressively claims the largest collection of telescopes for public viewing in the United States.

A quote from Worthington inscribed on the wall of his brewery articulates his invitation to pay attention to the here, right now. "What do *you* see when you look up at the night sky?" he asks, then answers, "I see two things. Like a Van Gogh on the wall of a museum, I see beautiful art, strange and humbling and constantly changing. I also see a reference point. Space travel is an understandable ambition. But to these eyes everything is too far away, too hot, too cold, too toxic, or too lifeless. The cosmos is a refreshing reminder of how lucky we are to live on such a unique planet. Truly, there's no place like home. Let's leave it better than we found it." I think Worthington is on to something. Perhaps the notion of cultural and educational offsets could be added to the mix of carbon offset options offered to companies around the world. If the chorus of "I love you, man! I love you, bro!" heard at breweries after a pint or two could be replaced with "I love you, planet! I love you, Milky Way!" we'd be on to something.

In addition to this clutch of education-oriented observatories in the high desert, there is an exciting national movement to combat light pollution, a celestial Nature Conservancy, a galactic ONDA if you will. It's the International Dark Sky Association. All around the world, dark sky communities are organizing; sky parks and reserves are being designated as sanctuaries for dark sky protection. Oregon astronomer Bill Kowalik is behind the central Oregon effort: "Several of us are involved in quantitative measurement of the skyglow in central Oregon, to provide a baseline of the current situation. We plan to periodically re-measure the skyglow to assess changes. We are in the process of bootstrapping an Oregon-wide chapter of the International Dark Sky Association. The Oregon chapter will work to stave off light pollution and bring back the starry skies." In Bend, it's Lights Out, Bend, with volunteers lobbying for fewer and less bright lights in town.

Oregon is home to one of the largest and highest quality dark sky zones and statewide has some of the darkest skies in the United States. According to astronomer Kirina Riggins, the last and most southeastern section of the Oregon Desert Trail, through the Owyhee Canyonlands, is one of the darkest areas in the country. Kowalik and his associates are concerned that this celestial treasure is at risk from encroaching light pollution. "Oregonians working together can reverse the light pollution trend and preserve our dark sky heritage," he says. It is striking, looking at the overall map of the ODT, how perfectly the trail mirrors the areas of Oregon's high-desert skies that the International Dark Sky Association proposes for protection. Indeed, the Milky Way is the trekker's shroud each night on the Oregon Desert Trail, its gauzy haze seemingly something you can touch, a fairy dust you can inhale, a gossamer hammock that rocks our earthbound world with incomprehensible concepts of time and space.

The dark sky movement joins other movements with similarly urgent and poignant goals, such as identifying and protecting locations where one can stand for fifteen minutes and not hear a man-made sound, which is becoming harder and harder to find. We're more familiar with other initiatives—returning fisheries and coral reefs to health and ridding the oceans of plastics, where instead of a musky tangle of kelp, a line of discarded plastics records the high mark of the most recent record-breaking moon tide. We are drawing conservation and preservation lines in the sand of Oregon's high desert and, too, in sound waves, sky, and water.

✦

Pine Mountain Observatory's telescopes bring stargazers up close and personal with a light show of amazing proportions: meteor showers, nebulae, the late-arriving news of star births and deaths, and eclipse events. Central Oregon was along the path of totality during the 2017 eclipse. What a high-desert sight it was—the eclipse itself, of course, but equally impressive the chill in the air during the eclipse, the silence of the birds, the chastening realization as to how quickly we'd be toast without the sun. No one was unaffected. Hundreds of social media posts told the story. Here are two:

"You get an overwhelming sense of humbleness and how small and petty we really are compared to the mechanics of the solar system, the clockwork of the universe. These events that are taking place, that in no way can we affect or stop. It gives us a sense of how tiny we are and yet how we're connected to the whole system. All this happens all at once."—Fred Espenak

"I saw the total eclipse and I realized that I was living in a much deeper, much more dynamic universe than I had previously considered."—David Makepeace

Nature has been tapping on our shoulders politely, asking to cut in on our self-absorbed dance. The tapping is turning into a pounding as we, oblivious, continue to move across the dance floor, unheeding. Seriously, what will it take? The eclipse brought us to our knees in a shared, though fleeting, recognition of how big and extraordinary nature is, that it *rules*. How about being as moved by our daily, small-scale experiences—dawn, sunset, thunderstorms, baby scrub jays fledging noisily in the front yard?

The more mundane but noteworthy headline associated with the 2017 eclipse was the inability of the central Oregon region to accommodate the hordes who came despite months of intergovernmental planning involving law enforcement agencies, BLM, Forest Service, municipalities, and counties. Hundreds of thousands descended on the high desert to witness the eclipse. Highways were in gridlock for miles and hours as swarms of people, seventy thousand in one high-desert meadow, congregated on BLM or Forest Service areas, putting extraordinary pressure on the land as well as public and commercial services.

The hordes that overwhelmed the region that day felt like a foreboding, a prophesy of what central Oregon, growing in popularity, will be up against as more and more seek out its rugged beauty. Are we trying to prevent people from coming? Or encouraging them but telling them what to do and when and where? And according to whom?

FIVE

Haints

PINE MOUNTAIN IS not only an invitation to look up but also to look out. Before strapping on your knapsack and heading south toward Christmas Valley, find a good perch on the top of the hill above the observatory and gaze out at the expanse. This was the traditional home of the Northern Paiutes who moved through this part of the high desert, leaving fire circles, taking shelter in caves where they wove moccasins from sage bark, scraped hair off the hides of deer and antelope to make clothing. Look for still-visible scars on the steep hillsides made by early white settlers who'd tie a tree on the back of their mule-drawn wagons to slow the perilous descent. Picture the desert towns that sprang up during the Homestead Acts, now gone without a trace.

After the Northern Paiutes had been driven off their tribal lands, the wars and skirmishes over, the influx of white settlers into the high desert gained momentum. In the mid-1800s the best of the land, acreage with water, was sought after by those traveling on the Oregon Trail.

In his book *The Meek Cutoff*, historian Brooks Ragen follows a group of more than a thousand men, women, and children who fell prey to a version of today's border "coyote," trusting an unknown guide to lead them across the desert to the promised land of the lush Willamette Valley. It was well known that the route from Idaho over the Blue Mountains to western Oregon was treacherous. Seeking a more manageable and faster passage two hundred wagons with livestock in tow cast their lot with a fast-talking fur trapper, Stephen Meek, who claimed to know a shortcut through the high desert.

Ragen describes the forty-day ordeal that resulted in illness and, for some, death, before making it only as far as Bend. Meek mistook the profile of Steens Mountain as that of the Cascades and led the group farther and farther west, deeper into the sage and rock, farther and farther from food and water. ODT trekkers might unwittingly step over unmarked graves, walk across fossilized wagon tracks, or kick up a mule shoe thrown while traversing the rough country. Did Stephen Meek not have a compass? Was he not able to read the night sky? Had he no knowledge of geographical features? On Friday, September 12, 1845, an emigrant wrote in his journal that "famine seemed inevitable. We were all starving and sick, were out of Food, eating emigrant cattle made many sick, the suffering was intense, we had no bread for weeks. If anything will try a person it is hardship such as we endured."

Sixty years after the hapless Meek wagon train, from your present-day perch on Pine Mountain, you'd likely see giant, roiling clouds of dry topsoil. Some old-timers remember days in the early 1900s when the sun was obscured by dust on the drive between Bend and Burns.

It wasn't drought or the high desert's version of the Dust Bowl; those roiling clouds of fine, chalky topsoil were caused by hundreds of horses on the move. "Along the road a person could see five thousand at once," an old buckaroo once told me. "And every one of 'em belonged to Bill Brown." It was said Bill Brown owned more horses than anyone in the West. His Horseshoe Bar brand was blazoned on horseflesh running from Oregon's Fort Rock to Wagontire, from Gilchrist Valley to Alkali Lake.

Brown benefited from what was not claimed during homesteading efforts—acre upon acre of ground considered useless, nonarable, and unpalatable except to native fauna, cows, and sheep. These lands were a big problem for a federal government that did not want to be in the business of managing large tracts of what it considered inhospitable, good-for-nothing high-desert rangeland. The Forest Service, started in 1891 as the Forest Reserve Act, was proving job enough. The hope was an opportunity would arise to address the need to off-load more of the lands in its care.

Until it did, the unclaimed expanses of the high desert suited the ambitions of this loner dubbed the "Horse King That Walked." Despite all the horses he owned, he only rode if there was no other option, preferring to go on foot, a book in his back pocket. "Time for reading worthwhile books and doing worthwhile thinking," he was known to say. Whistling to himself, he'd happily walk the desert for days. His ranch hands claimed he could outwalk any saddle horse. Cowboys said on the rare occasions he rode, he would run his horse until it was completely winded and then get off and lead his mount twice the distance they had just covered at a gallop. More than likely it was Farewell, his loyal and long-suffering favorite mare, who tolerated this unusual treatment. A prophetic choice in name, for ultimately Bill Brown would be forced to say goodbye to his beloved desert and to his most cherished dreams. But there was no foreshadowing of that sad ending at the turn of the twentieth century.

Raised in western Oregon, Bill Brown and two of his brothers got their start in 1882 in Wagontire raising sheep, and by 1920, Bill had bought out his brothers and owned eight bands of roughly a thousand ewes each. Many confirm he often trailed behind his bands, walking twenty miles in one day, and that he carried strychnine in one pocket to poison coyotes and raisins or dried prunes in the other to provide himself with some sustenance. Folks liked to tell stories about Bill getting the pockets mixed up or mixing the two in the same pocket. A good yarn, but just not so. Ingesting even a trace of strychnine would have killed him.

In 1903 the *Prineville Review* quaintly reported that five hundred of Bill's sheep were slaughtered by Paulina sharpshooters using "the bullet method." The range wars subsided in 1906 when the US government stepped in and assigned allotments specific to sheep and cattle on the unclaimed homestead offerings that were eventually consolidated to form the Bureau of Land Management.

But never mind the welcome truce between sheep- and cattlemen, and never mind the ongoing profits Brown continued to make from selling his wool. He was already playing a new hunch. For years big cities across the United States had used draft horses to pull trolleys. When electricity was introduced in the 1890s, hundreds of horses suddenly flooded the market. Bill bought all he could. Just because it seemed like a good idea. Just because he thought big and small at once—"largely" as he put it. Just because he was "morally certain" there would be a use for them. "Half genius and half damn fool," was how he was described.

In addition to the horses he purchased, he had his cowboys chase down, corral, and brand as many of the horses they could find that ran wild in the high desert. Some were said to be descendants of stock that arrived in 1514 with Cortés from Spain. Ranchers joked that these horses weren't wild at all, but rather ranchers' discards turned out in the desert to fend for themselves.

At his peak Brown had over seven thousand horses that ranged across southeastern and central Oregon. These numbers were, without question, very hard on the land, but his timing was uncanny. The year 1898 marked the war with Spain. Representatives of the US Army cavalry traveled to central Oregon to purchase horses from Brown. Then came the Boer War, from 1899 to 1902, and Bill subsequently found a willing buyer in the British Army, which continued to use cavalry in World War I. Brown was selling the horses he had bought at seven dollars each for eighty-seven dollars each. All this time he was running on essentially unregulated land. But the Horse King's luck was about to run out.

With the start of the mass production of the automobile in 1913 and the end of the First World War in 1918, Bill's horses were no longer needed. By 1931 he was reduced to selling them for dog and chicken feed—or for "pony coats." By 1935 everything he had worked for was gone. He was placed in an old persons' domiciliary in Salem, Oregon, where he gave all the residents shovels and exhorted them to get out of their rockers and dig up the grounds for planting potatoes, all the while muttering his oft-repeated mantra: "Work hard from cradle to grave." He tried more than once to escape, to walk back to the desert from Salem, back to his beloved Buck Creek. In 1941 Bill Brown died in the domiciliary at age eighty-five. One old Horseshoe Bar mare was last seen in 1953 wandering the high desert, muzzle white from age. Maybe it was Farewell.

✦

Meanwhile, back at the ranch, so to speak, the opportunity to unload more of the unclaimed lands in the high desert that the federal government had long been waiting for had finally arrived in central Oregon in the form of the railroad. Until 1911, the year the Oregon Trunk Line of the Great Northern Railway pulled into Bend, the region had the dubious honor of being the largest territory in the United States without rail transportation, according to George Putnam, who started Bend's first newspaper a year earlier. As railroad baron James J. Hill drove the golden spike into Bend's soil on that auspicious October day, none cheered louder than the federal government, who saw the arrival of the iron horse as a golden opportunity to rid themselves of their favorite migraine: unwanted land.

Historian and photographer Rich Bergeman who, in 2016, toured an exhibit of his photographs of homesteads in the high desert, is quoted as describing this last land rush as the government's effort "to settle the worst, last land in the West." Shameless, trumped-up efforts were again used to persuade unwitting wanna-be landowners to make a home in the high and dry. Leaflets promised a farmer's paradise, the next great agriculture empire of the United States, the Palouse of the high desert! With the last Homestead Acts of 1909 and 1912, settlers were lured by the promise of acreage touted by land locaters as the "prairies" of central Oregon. The offer was even extended to single women over the age of twenty-one, an equal opportunity established as early as the Homestead Act of 1862. Of the tens of thousands who were granted parcels through the Homestead Acts, a notable 18 percent were single women.

Alice Day Pratt was one, and she outlasted most of the men. In 1900 she proved up on 160 acres near Post, Oregon, the geographic center of the state, holding on to her small claim, garden, twenty cows and Leghorn chickens for nearly two decades before returning, destitute, to the skyscraper canyons of New York City. The in-migration peaked in the fall of 1911 when the Enlarged Homestead Act increased the number of acres from 160 to 320. The filing fee was reduced to ten dollars, buying the unwitting a chance to start over and to secure land all their own, a place to raise a family. It also served to bring the government that much closer to its goal of priva-tizing vast, dry, windy, unwanted expanses. At least that was the idea. Though Alice Day Pratt's time in the high desert was long on hard-ship, in her journal she nevertheless summed up her experience this way: "I have been cold and hungry and ragged and penniless. I have been free and strong and buoyant and glad." Alice was the exception.

From your perch on Pine Mountain you are looking not only at the ghosts of nomadic Northern Paiutes, of the Horse King's herds, of abandoned small ranches and farms, but also, after the last Home-stead Act, at the sites of whole towns now vanished—the silenced heartbeats of the schools, stores, dance halls, and post offices of Rolyat, Imperial, Stauffer, Dry Lake, and Fife that were once strung like pearls of false hope across the high desert. Imperial, near Pine Mountain, was one of the more elaborate land swindles of the time with many buying into false claims of abundant water. Stauffer briefly had a village newspaper. Dairy farms! Even dairy farms were valiantly attempted. On your thru-hike you might find a rotting cor-ral post leaning toward the ground or a desiccated, tangled clump of thorny matrimony vine clinging to a weathered board, once part of a homesteader's kitchen wall. Women emptied the kitchen wash basin out the window to water the hardy vine in order to have some hint of greenery in the desolate landscape. But more substantial evi-dence of the many lives laid on the line there isn't.

In a cruel joke of nature, conditions were wetter than usual in the 1900s. Homesteaders were optimistic the promises made by the locaters would be promises kept and put their shoulders to the plow. But reality soon set bone-grindingly in. This was indeed a desert. And a high one at that, affording very little rain and a limited growing season, with freezes a given every month of the year. And then there was the wind. Author E. R. Jackman paints a bleak picture of homesteaders in the area near Pine Mountain in *The Oregon Desert*.

> Scientists say that man can adapt to any kind of weather except continuous wind. Unremitting, unrelenting wind blows ambition right out of a man, leaving him without hope or plan. In the winter, it can kill him, just by blowing away his heat, and in the summer, it can kill his soul. The homesteader's houses, of board and batten, couldn't hold out a determined wind, and many a man came in from his day's work to find his wife crying hysterically as she looked at a dish of mashed potatoes, too covered with dust to reveal its identity. The desert was awful hard on horses and women.

By 1930, all but 9 percent of those who'd arrived between 1908 and 1915 had thrown in the towel. Larger ranches took over some of the claims that were never proved up but the rest, the driest, the least desirable, went back to the federal government, faced with no choice but to adopt the unwanted acres left in a basket on its doorstep. The large tracts were put in the hands of what was then called the General Land Office, which eventually morphed into the Bureau of Land Management in 1946. The government, as Jackman pointed out, tried to give away the land "for seventy years with no takers." This excerpt from "The Old Ranch Mother" by Sharlot M. Hall helps explain why.

> Long time ago I used to say to Jim,
> ('Fore any children come to call him Paw.)
> "Oh Jim, oh Jim, let's leave this sorry place
> An' go where trees is, an' green grass,
> An' water springs. This desert here
> Burns up my heart an' makes me so afraid.
> Let's go where folks is—Jim, oh Jim, let's go."
> An' Jim, he'd chaw an' spit an' chaw,
> An' say: "Aw, Lizy, this place it's all right:
> The cattle's company better'n too much folks."

From your Pine Mountain vantage point today you can just see the silhouette of a small cluster of abandoned buildings next to Highway 20. It's a town trying hard not to be a ghost. Named after a cattle rancher and miner who settled in the area in the 1880s, Millican opened a post office in 1913 to serve a population of sixty. By 1940, Millican's official population had dropped to one. That would be the postmaster who ran things from 1922 to 1945. When he left, the post office closed. Next was a man who kept the store and unincorporated town going for forty-two years until he was shot in cold blood by his sole employee, a parolee from the Oregon State Penitentiary. Millican (what was the store, the hollowed-out shell of a gas station and garage, a two-unit motel of sorts, a house and corral and seventy-four acres) has been through a variety of owners since and is again for sale—for $1,499,000 you can own it. It's touted as a one-hundred-space RV park with unrivaled sunset views! An ideal location to grow and sell marijuana (thanks to Oregon's legalization of pot and the current zoning)! Close to mountain biking and dirt biking trails! Adjacent to the Central Oregon Shooting Sports Range! Near the Oregon Badlands Wilderness! The next bedroom community of Bend (give or take twenty years)! And speaking of desert myths, in a humorous article about Millican, author Janet Eastman of the *Oregonian* suggests the store reopen and feature what used to be its best-selling product: Bouncing Bunny unsweetened jackrabbit milk, "a balanced diet for unbalanced people, rich in vitamins J, U, M, and P."

Fast-forward from the homesteading days to the recession of 2008 and the snake oil promises made about the affordability of a home, ARMs, mortgages, and loans, all too good to be true. Green lawns in parched deserts, picket fences, perfect children, and Norman Rockwell as your neighbor. As the housing market collapsed and mortgages were called, our century's version of ghost towns were created daily; modern-day swindlers were exposed. A young friend of mine living in the California desert told me about the Armageddon-like aftermath he witnessed. I can't get it out of my head as I reflect on our inclination to do the same thing over and over and expect a different result. He described brand-new housing developments completely abandoned, not a soul to be seen other than, here and there, an opportunistic skateboarder. In parched backyards, dust devils played with the loose, dry dirt; the trademark swimming pools were full of putrid water, and in them, bloated and floating, abandoned dogs and cats who had succumbed to their thirst. All ground cover and shrubs had been removed during construction of these pop-up neighborhoods, so there was no birdsong to soften the edges of the tragedy—instead, an alien chirping of distressed smoke alarms emanating from house after house. Bend was the national poster child for foreclosures during this time. Houses were seized and put on the auction block. Investors walked away from half-completed developments, leaving the high-desert winds to play through skeletal two-by-four fantasies of home.

Nothing is starker than an abandoned housing development in the desert: the scarring created by piping and utility lines, roads leading nowhere, tattered lot-line flags, half-finished structures standing naked on the treeless horizon, opportunistic cheatgrass welcoming the disruption of soil and claiming new territory. Nothing is more desperate, that is, unless it's abandoned homes or incomplete housing developments anywhere else, everywhere else.

What ghost towns are we creating now? Look at us go! What natural or manmade resource do we believe will never give out? What communities are being shuttered in the aftermath of changing economics? Newly minted ghost towns come online across the nation every day as we buy into the same worn-out lines used in the days of the Homestead Act. Land! Water! Jobs! Unlimited this and that! Bend and Deschutes County are among the top ten fastest growing in the entire nation. The *New York Times* no longer refers to "Bend, Oregon" in its articles, but simply "Bend" as if it were Seattle or Denver or San Francisco. Open spaces and resources, beware.

Those of us who have lived in the region for any length of time see the changes in climate and the effects of population growth. But young newcomers feel they have "discovered" this wonderful area based on modern-day hawkers of promise and prosperity. They write not only their personal history but the region's starting the moment they land, the beginning of time and history. It's age-(in)appropriate. We all did this. The new arrivals are ambitious and energetic, and they're here to prove up on their claim: a job that affords them and their family a house with a plot of ground to go with it. But we, our lives, are constructs, as temporary as the efforts of the homesteaders. Our unchecked ambitions are rendered in graphic relief against the high desert's dispassionate background. Nothing lasts. Nothing. And no fact keeps us on the run to prove it wrong like that one does. This is why conservation is so hard. It means looking at history repeating itself in the eye. It means thinking more of future generations than self, the ultimate delayed gratification. It means imagining *moi* gone, out of the picture. Most of us would rather be lemmings than proactive leaders. Most of us would rather sleepwalk than stay awake, rather pretend immortality than take action to preserve a world for the seventh generation.

WEST BASIN AND RANGE

*To me it's a thru-hike in an isolated place that promotes
a conversation in land management, ethics, and usage.
Hiking across a vast and remote landscape and having a
random and chance encounter with cowboys and hunters
to discuss how "all of us" should treat the land, how we all
have a responsibility, no matter our political leanings, really
showed me the pulse of people in rural areas especially here
out West.*

THRU-HIKER RYAN "DIRTMONGER" SYLVA

SIX

H₂OPE

O UR NEXT DESTINATION on the Oregon Desert Trail as it transitions from the Central Oregon Volcanics to the West Basin and Range is Christmas Valley, reputedly named after pioneer cattleman Peter Christman. It is the setting for another (my favorite) high-desert land-rush story. Currently claiming a population of thirteen hundred, it was 1955 before the community got electricity. It's located an inconvenient thirty miles from the nearest highway in the Oregon Outback and nearly twice that distance on the ODT from Pine Mountain. The sagebrush ocean that envelops this outpost laps against the two paved roads that bisect the town, where tumbleweed, head-over-heeling down the streets, is the closest thing to traffic. In the distance, otherworldly volcanic formations (Fort Rock and Table Rock) dominate the skyline or pock the ground in the form of enormous craters (Hole in the Ground), evidence of when the land was on molten fire. Nineteen miles of nothing to the north and east is Fossil Lake, where, in 2018, forty-three-thousand-year-old tracks of

Columbian mammoths were discovered, the imprints describing the herds' arduous trek across a frigid and frozen central Oregon.

Walking through the endless, immutable sage flats can some-times cause a sort of vertigo, can feel like a sage-out, no up, no down, no end, alone and adrift in this sagebrush ocean with hues that mimic the pastels of the sunsetting sky. But to California real estate developer M. Penn Phillips, the miles of sage were a field of dreams. Christmas Valley, he decided, would be the Palm Desert of Oregon. In 1959 he bought seventy-two thousand acres and built an airport, an A-frame lodge with a restaurant and bar, an artificial lake, a golf course, and a water system. Damn if he didn't sell close to all of that land in the first few months. Predictions were that the popu-lation of Christmas Valley would reach five thousand. In what is by now a familiar tactic perfected by land locators during the home-steading years, he promoted the development with a string of super-latives: agricultural nirvana, a perfect destination for hobby farmers (never mind that at that time there was precious little arable ground available and that if farmers weren't making it on five thousand acres, forty- and twenty-acre allotments weren't likely to cut it). A year later, with only 150 living on their "claims," Phillips called it quits. He deserves credit for the fact that his unbridled enthusiasm sparked the creation of Christmas Valley's first school. Other traces of his effort that remain include the lodge, golf course, manmade lake, and the names he assigned to the streets: Holly, Glitter, Snowman, Noel, Christmas Tree. To encounter these street names when the temperature is a hundred degrees and a hot, dusty wind is blowing is odd, to say the least. Slightly more reality based would have been to choose names inspired by the water the area used to claim: Marsh, Liquid Gold, Inland Sea, Ripple. Go back far enough, to the Pleisto-cene, and Fort Rock Lake covered 1,260 square miles and was three hundred feet deep, covering Christmas and Fort Rock valleys. In fact, the whole of the Great Basin was a land of vast lakes and lush forests. Giant beavers, bison, and camels roamed the lakes' shores. Now, the best the region can do is ghost lakes: dry lake beds, seasonal playas. Where did all that water go?

Christmas Valley's newspaper is called the *Community Breeze*. Considering the gales that regularly blow through this part of the world, that's an understatement. My take is that the inspiration for the weekly's name is based on the fact that Terry Crawford—*Breeze* owner, editor, reporter, printer, advertising manager, and distributor— makes everything look like a breeze: managing her horses, her property, and her family, while running the paper and serving on every committee in town. High octane, involved, engaged. Why Christmas Valley?

Her reasoning is typical of those who remained after the failed development in the '60s and of subsequent arrivals. Space. Quiet. Tight-knit community. Land. The sense that you are part of something bigger, that man and nature are in balance, one with the other. In Christmas Valley, in the high desert, neither nature nor man are over-dancing their partner.

What is the appeal of small, rural communities? Ask Portland poet Penelope Schambly Schott who bought a house as a writing getaway in Dufur, Oregon (population 630), located above the Columbia River. Known for its farms that stretch in every direction across an undulating horizon of wheat, Dufur holds an annual Threshing Bee that reenacts early, laborious harvesting techniques now accomplished with huge combines. The tiny downtown is as crisp, clean, and angular as the farmers' fields. Based on her Dufur experience, Schott has concluded that in small-town conversations everyone's name is followed by their function: *the* accountant, farmer, rancher, floozy, welder, plumber, drunk, newspaper editor, and now, eccentric poet. In Dufur, in Christmas Valley, in all small communities everywhere, it's easy to identify a problem and readily fix it. There's little bureaucracy. All are held as able. Slackers needn't apply. In a little pond, any well-intentioned small fish can be a huge positive, a game changer. There's a certain appeal to this.

When Terry Crawford invited me to be one of three keynote speakers at the 2018 Christmas Valley Gala Dinner put on by the Chamber of Commerce, I was serving as executive director of PLAYA, a residency campus for artists and scientists located sixty-nine miles south. I had gotten to know her because, rain or shine, Terry Crawford was a loyal attendee at the monthly PLAYA Presents, when resident artists and scientists open their studios to the public.

Other than hiking iconic landmarks (Fort Rock, Hole in Ground, Crack in the Ground) adjacent to the ODT, what I knew of Christmas Valley at that point was limited to a couple of visits to this north Lake County town to talk up PLAYA as a cultural resource for the community. On one trip I met with some women involved in the local schools to discuss the possibility of PLAYA residents doing workshops at the middle and high school levels. We had lunch at the lodge, the centerpiece of the failed development. It had been reopened and refurbished only a few months before, one of the town's encouraging signs of renewed health. There are others: Christmas Valley now has a medical clinic for thru-trekkers should they need a shin splint treatment or tick bite exam, a new high school with a brand-new track, a grocery store, a library, various churches, and lodging options with hot showers for weary thru-hikers. After lunch, while exploring the main street, I discovered Willows Antiques, with two outlets bookending the town on the east and west. I passed signs posted by real estate agents hawking thousands of acres of potential farmland or, alternatively, a third of an acre big enough for a single wide, a "Home Sweet Home" sign beckoning.

Here, anyone can have what defines wealth across the world: land. And many will go to great lengths to hang on to their piece of turf. A woman I met works multiple jobs requiring her to drive hundreds of miles a day to support her acreage and animals in what most would see as a desolate, wind-blown community. Juxtaposed with the absentee farmers whose industrial-sized alfalfa operations are a trademark of the valley, the gigantic fields prowled by massive prehistoric-looking center-pivot sprinklers that spew as much as thirty gallons of water a minute during the growing season—and we're up close and personal with the haves and have-nots. Or are we? Regardless of net worth, those I spoke to who live in Christmas Valley feel they have influence and relevance and they own land. They feel they're in on a secret they are very glad the rest of the world hasn't heard about or wouldn't be tempted by if they did: the astounding privilege of living out.

When I arrived at the chamber gala the mood was festive. Seemingly out of nowhere people materialized in their cars and big diesel pickups. Everyone was dressed up. Inside the lodge restaurant, a table sagged under the weight of raffle and silent auction items: certificates for a dinner at the lodge, a free ad in the *Community Breeze*, a side of beef, antelope sausage, lube/oil/filter at the local garage, massage, hair styling, an elk tag for hunters in the mix, of which there were many. A basket of homemade jams and condiments was displayed next to another filled with home décor items from Willows Antiques. "I'm lonely and available," joked the woman tending bar. The eight table rounds of ten quickly filled. The other two dinner speakers included the superintendent of North County Schools and a woman from La Pine, a growing community outside of Bend, there to talk about potential tourism opportunities that had worked for La Pine and might work in Christmas Valley. Terry Crawford was the emcee. The whole evening was wonderful theater, staged on the vast empty. I felt and feel as at home with a roomful of people who hang their hats on a rural way of life as I do anywhere, people who live close to the land, whose lives are dictated by seasons and weather. Maybe it's as simple as the kinship felt among those passionate about something, the same thing, willing to lay their lives on the line for it. In this case, a great big wide sagebrush-studded flat.

I used my five minutes to invite the community to take better advantage of PLAYA: free transportation from Christmas Valley to the monthly PLAYA Presents, featuring presentations or performances by resident musicians, writers, and scientists. Community conversations led by resident artists and scientists were also part of the monthly program, but when I listed the possible topics they might address, I did not include water. It would be like insulting your best friend's mother. This valley's water issues echo those being grappled with everywhere—be they lack of fresh water, uncontaminated water, or rising sea levels. The elephant in the room, in all rooms everywhere, is water. Maybe if it's not discussed, it doesn't exist.

I am reminded of Ursula Le Guin's parable "The Ones Who Walk Away from Omelas." Omelas is a place where it's guaranteed that everyone in the town can live happily and have all they ever dreamed of having. No poverty, no rancor, no hardship, so long as they're okay with the fact that a single child, just one, is kept in perpetual filth, isolation, darkness, and misery. That's the trade-off. Some walk away from Omelas upon learning about this bargain with the devil. But most stay.

✦

The Horse King Bill Brown settled on Buck Creek as his high-desert headquarters. Given all the picture-perfect valleys he could choose from, why that location? Bill Brown intuited that if he controlled the water, he controlled the high desert. What Brown was after were the locations that had springs and creeks. In those days Buck Creek ran year-round. He speculated the water could be moved from where it was to where it was needed, and he was right. Bill Brown country is still laced with his handmade ditches and rock-lined aqueducts that hug the sides of hills and coulees and carried water to fields and pasturelands. Hikers might come across one walking the ODT. Access to fresh water has shaped civilization. In the high desert it has determined which lands were claimed and which languished under the BLM's management.

In Christmas Valley, the availability of underground water translated into economic opportunity in the form of large-scale alfalfa production for export and domestic use. Some claim those mega-farms have caused the water table in Christmas Valley to drop. Wells are being drilled deeper. Are the farms draining underground water reservoirs? Is there an imbalance in the recharge and discharge of water resources? Snowmelt, it's assumed, returns water through the soil and replenishes strained aquifers. With less and less annual average snow accumulation, that's not happening. We know it's not. Old-timers recall being able to haul a barge of fresh-cut logs across Summer Lake. Now the lake is maybe six inches deep and evaporates completely most summers.

Approximately twenty miles east of Christmas Valley is one of nature's anomalies, the Lost Forest, a stand of pine and juniper that has survived, it is estimated, for twelve thousand years despite dramatic shifts in climate that resulted in other forests heading for the hills and huge lakes receding and eventually vanishing. Now the Lost Forest is dying. Some blame recreational all-terrain enthusiasts who noisily jet across the delicate dunes throwing up rooster tails of sand, minerals, pumice, and ash shot from the caldera of Mazama. The dunes are important to the Lost Forest. The ash deposits soak up and conserve limited rainfall to nourish the ancient conifers. Others blame industrial farm operations for pumping the precious Pleistocene water, also referred to as fossil or paleo water, for which there is no replacement. Don't forget the increasingly prevalent patterns of drought. Don't forget the effect on vegetation and fauna that global warming is creating.

Peter Mehringer, emeritus professor of archaeology at the University of Washington and practiced in taking the long view, advocates calm. "As climate changes, vegetation changes. You have to look at this as one clip of one movie, and you have to look at the whole film." The long view of science, however, does nothing to calm those wanting water now, money in the bank now, jobs now; it does not quiet those demanding stricter regulations on water use now. The answer can only be a blend of the long and the short view to get to a workable, on-the-ground answer. Some high-desert cases in point.

1. In 2014 Oregon senator Jeff Merkley helped pass legislation that, by reallocating Prineville Reservoir storage releases, benefited Lower Crooked River fisheries, a good thing, and also benefited the new kid on the block, Facebook, which now claims 3.2 million square feet, making the Prineville, Oregon, data center the company's biggest anywhere. To secure and improve their small-town economies, rural communities across the country are promising the moon to corporations searching for a home. Sometimes the effect on adjacent, preexisting agrarian concerns is not fully factored in. Prineville is

grappling with this. All kinds of perks were offered to lure Facebook, and it worked, never mind that the actual number of permanent jobs Facebook has created in Prineville is only 350, that's nine thousand square feet per employee. Facebook uses mist to cool the air in its gargantuan center. Merkley's bill apparently did not take into account the impact altered reservoir storage releases would have upriver. According to a letter drafted by Upper Crooked River ranchers, the timing and quantity of the reallocations "compromise the vitality of the Upper Crooked River watershed by forcing early regulation of irrigation." The letter extrapolates that ultimately the forced early regulation would undermine the viability of Upper Crooked River ranches. Nothing like water issues to bring property owners to a, well, boil.

The Upper Crooked River, separated from the lower river by a reservoir, was negatively impacted in the 1990s when the Army Corps of Engineers responded to the flooding of the upper river by straightening it using big, brutish front-end loaders, the prevailing engineering answer to river flooding at that time. The straightened, accelerated water course resulted in severe bank erosion and the loss of marshlands that provided fish and wildlife habitat and the water storage the marshes created. A regional group in Crook County made up of hydrologists, ranchers, the Crook County Watershed Council, and Oregon State University representatives want to address the Upper and Lower Crooked River as one river, which of course it is. They seek to return the sinuosity to the Upper Crooked River so it can store and retain more water and thereby offset the new (and some feel unilaterally granted) demands for water below, including the insatiable appetite of modern technology. If you use Facebook, you are implicated in the Crooked River's health or lack thereof.

2. Tumalo, Oregon, has an irrigation district established at the beginning of the twentieth century. Ditches diverted water from Tumalo Creek and the Deschutes River and turned sage flats into productive ground. As Martin Winch observed in his book *Tumalo: A Thirsty Land*, historically "the semi-arid lands of the Tumalo area of central Oregon have drawn people to reclaim them into irrigated farms." In those days that meant small sheep or cattle ranches, dairies, and cropland. But Tumalo, like Prineville, also has a new kid on the block. A Tumalo dairyman, who has been getting up to milk his cows at a God-awful, pre-dawn hour his entire working life, good-naturedly questions, "Who's the dummy? Me, up at 3:00 a.m. for the last four decades to milk my cows or my new neighbor with his automated greenhouse making money hand over fist?" The new kid is cannabis, thanks to Oregon's legalization of marijuana production. Tumalo is particularly popular because until marijuana is legalized nationally, as hemp has been, growers aren't authorized to irrigate with water stored behind a federally built dam. Tumalo's dams are state built. The water rush is on! Gone are the days when the guy who wanted to hoard Tumalo water to create his own water ski lake was the Tumalo Irrigation District's biggest problem. With the advent of cannabis production, the district's job of water resource management just got much more interesting.

3. A well driller out of Prineville explained to me that modern drilling technology has a camera attached that records images as the probe augers deeper and deeper in search of water. He didn't have words to describe the impact on him of the images of vast, yawning, desiccated caverns of volcanic rock far underground. He speculated they were ancient waterways, now dry and exposed. The photos he showed me were like exotic underground nebulae, extravagant

flourishes of rock shaped by water and now marooned. "But," he assured me, "if we drill deep enough, we eventually get to water."

Jack Wilson, known as Wovoka, was a Paiute who created the Ghost Dance in the late nineteenth century, a popular pan-Indian spiritual movement that prophesized the end of white supremacy and the return to Native Americans of tribal lands. Among Paiutes he was also known for his reputed ability to control the weather and to end droughts. It's said he caused a block of ice to fall out of the sky on a summer day. The high desert needs him now.

I imagine enormous caverns being drained under Christmas Valley, the formations mimicking the unusual land formations above. Cities and towns across the United States, either because they are in deserts or because they are growing too fast or because of industrial pollution—or all three—have freshwater resource issues. Left unaddressed, I imagine all of us happily living in Omelas, eventually falling, literally and apocalyptically, into the caverns of our greed. I imagine giant sinkholes swallowing us whole. But before that happens, I imagine a gathering of those who care about water and care about resource management and the enterprises and lives that depend on the high desert's liquid gold. I imagine them coming up with solutions that work not just for this region but inform water resource management issues nationally, if not worldwide.

Leaving the cautionary water tale of Christmas Valley for Diablo Mountain, on the eastern side of Summer Lake, hikers can relax about the availability of water. How quickly we forget. The sight of water and we assume there is no shortage. Trekkers are about to encounter what has to be one of the most beautiful and arresting landscapes anywhere. The desert feigning lush extravagance: river, creeks, marshes, springs. Novelist-theologian Marilynne Robinson's

WEST BASIN AND RANGE

quote comes to mind: "Heaven is improbable, but how improbable is this existence?" Included in "this existence," as far as I'm concerned, is the perfect ordering of escarpment and basin, color and texture that surrounds this playa. Hikers will have traveled approximately 123 dry miles before getting to the shores of Summer Lake, where the lack of water seems a bad dream. Even so, individually and collectively we must think and imagine beyond our immediate physical, emotional, and cultural landscapes. We must do what is meet and right in conserving and caring even when we are walking through a perceived land of abundance.

SEVEN

Vapor Trails

AT THIS POINT on the trail you're likely to begin channeling your inner mystic. It's not heatstroke. It's not delirium. It's the effect of this magical section of the Oregon Desert Trail. "How much have I confused the coyote by peeing on his territory?" you might find yourself asking, or "Who am I?" *Tat twam*, "Thou art that," in Sanskrit. Welcome to the unreality of reality, the world of ellipses. Beware of odd impulses, such as setting up your GoPro in the middle of the lake bed, as one ecstatic traveler did, then running and leaping and twirling, stark naked, back and forth in front of the camera, getting farther and farther away, dancing, dancing what a life does, dancing, dancing a definition of infinity. Mother Nature as psychedelic. Notice how, increasingly, you are thinking "like an ion," as the reader board on the Summer Lake Store encourages. Or, as poet David Whyte asks, "How do you know you're on your path? Because it disappears. That's how."

Looking across Summer Lake is like viewing a kinetic exhibit of Mark Rothko paintings, long horizontal bands of color that change minute to minute depending on the movement of clouds, the position of the sun, the presence or absence of water in this seasonal five by fifteen miles of lake. If by now you haven't been brought to your knees by the perfection of nature, reminded of your relative place in the scheme of things—this section of the trail will take care of that.

Choreographed by the mercurial winds, alkaline dust devils gyrate and hula across the flat clay stage. Water, bullied by breezes, appears and disappears, the water line rising and falling willy-nilly. The doleful call of the whippet, gargle of raven, bugle of sandhill crane, howl of coyote and, yes, wolf punctuate the air. Family quarrels between the high scarps and ridges produce rain, lightning, and howling gusts of wind hurled back and forth that send black bear and cougar running for cover. The air is electric with energy. Walking under the brow of Diablo Mountain, its gentle slopes shaped by wave action eons ago, we're guests of a place and space where mountains walk and rocks inch across dry lake bottoms. True story. The surface of the claylike, dried playa appears brittle. But underneath, where there is moisture, it is stretching and cracking the surface. That cracking action slowly moves what sits atop its wizened gray elephant hide–like surface in one direction or another. Like restless legs at night, subcutaneous crawling. Yearning. An itch to move, to migrate, to shift, to explore—like all of us.

Dry lakes, or playas, are the result of evaporation seasonally exceeding recharge. Walking the shores of Summer Lake you get the impression you are next to or walking into a lung of the earth or inside its heart: the slo-mo pulsing and pumping, the bellows action of water present and water absent, now you see it and now you don't. The concentration of alkali means the lake itself is devoid of vegetation, so no fish. The water in this beautiful but faux oasis is not potable. There's some brine that waterfowl like, plus the lake is ringed with plants that provide critical habitat, so birds do linger, but the real avian concentration is found at the north end of the Summer Lake Wildlife Area, a vast thirty-square-mile checkerboard of dikes and marshes fed by the spring-fed Ana River. There are amenities at the town of Summer Lake, and the wildlife area has many accessible campgrounds, making it a worthy rival, in my book, of the better-known Malheur National Wildlife Refuge for access to viewing sites, the variety of birds moving through, and the beauty of the setting. Note to hikers: There's great swimming in the Ana Reservoir before you get lost on purpose somewhere on the east side of the lake.

It's easy to think you're the first and only one here as you move alone across this section of the ODT, but you're not. Instead, you're retracing the vapor trails of those who came before you: ancient animals (such as Pleistocene camels), prehistoric birds (today's sandhill crane has been around for 2.5 million years), or ancient insects (giant beetles with large, bony mandibles). Once the mandibles were removed, these juicy, crunchy beetle bodies were apparently a delicacy to those living in the Paisley caves fifteen thousand years ago, the earliest inhabitants of North America. According to findings by archaeologist Dr. Dennis Jenkins of the University of Oregon, the Paisley people lived on the Diablo Mountain side of Summer Lake. At that time the area was abounding in waterfowl, fish, large herds of grazing animals, and yes, beetles. Dr. Jenkins's exuberance and enthusiasm about his ongoing Paisley Cave Project research (and life in general) would lead one to think he just happened on to both. That the definitive evidence of Paisley man's existence was found by Dr. Jenkins in coprolites, a fancy name for desiccated poop, provides no end of comic material for this jovial and brilliant researcher. Trekkers can stand inside the shelter of the Paisley caves and imagine looking out across a vast inland sea called Lake Chewaucan, what is now Summer Lake and, to the south, Lakes Abert and Goose. The view captivated Bend-based videographer and photographer Scott Nelson, who was moved to put down his camera and pen this "word painting" in the form of a Japanese haibun, a brief observation of place written in prose and concluding with a haiku.

There is a cave north of Paisley, Oregon, where, 15,000 years ago, tribes traced to Asia and Africa crossed the Bering Strait and made their way to central Oregon. Climb the cliffs, enter the void, touch the soil, feel their presence. Imagine this was shelter as they gazed out across a vast inland sea, now forever dry.

Bones of a camel
litter the back of the cave,
take me back in time.

Tracing trails made by the earliest inhabitants, in this compressed history of braided intersecting pathways, you walk across their trade routes, their trails to hunting grounds and sacred sites and favored sources of root and berry for sustenance, reeds and marsh grasses for basketry. You step through teepee circles where hides were stretched, dried, and divined into cradle boards, where tools were cajoled out of bones.

You happen upon early homesteaders' pathways to the woodpile, or wagon tracks through orchards that dotted the valleys along Summer Lake in the early days of ranching and farming, or trails made by cattle as they were herded to summer pasture at higher elevations. Don't be surprised if the infamous and audacious ghost Princess Foster, the wife of one of the early ranchers on Summer Lake, visits your campsite, hides your compass and binoculars, and makes off with your granola bars or cap.

You intersect the route recorded by Captain John Frémont and others on his mapping expedition team. In 1843 army topographers spent three cold, miserable December nights during a whiteout on a windswept, snow-covered ridge before struggling down steep cliffs to reach what must have looked like a mirage: a large lake in the valley below. Frémont was moved to name the snow-covered rim Winter Ridge and the warm waters Summer Lake. This is the land of the largest fault-block mountains in the United States, and they will dominate the landscape until the terminus of the ODT. These dramatic uplifts also mean the presence of hot springs—to hikers' delight—starting with the springs on the south end of Summer Lake and followed by Hunters, Hart Mountain, Alvord, and the hot springs pools that are secluded within the Owyhee Canyonlands.

At our feet . . . more than a thousand feet below . . . we looked into a green prairie country, in which a beautiful lake, some twenty miles in length, was spread along the foot of the mountain. . . . Shivering in snow three feet deep, and stiffening in a cold north wind, we exclaimed at once that the names of summer lake and winter ridge should be applied to these proximate places of such sudden and violent contrast.

John C. Frémont
16 December 1843
Report, Second Expedition

John Frémont and I go way back. For a number of years, I lived in a house in Bend built in the 1930s. One summer a leak developed in the sixty-year-old water line, so I hired a contractor to dig up the old pipe and replace it. After days of backbreaking work, a five-foot-deep trench stretched from the street to within a few feet of my house. The contractor arrived that morning eager to complete the final section. I stated my usual request: "Be on the lookout for arrowheads!" I always believed moving dirt within view of the Deschutes River would produce evidence of the Columbia River tribes and Northern Paiutes who hunted and fished those banks hundreds of years before. I was at work at my desk when the contractor knocked on the door. "Get a load of this," he said.

What he held up was not an ancient mortar and pestle or glistening obsidian arrowhead but a round, rust-covered ball. "Looks like a cannonball! What if it's a cannonball!" he exclaimed. Our first course of excited action was to get someone to examine it and make sure it wouldn't detonate. I can't remember who performed that task or what, if any, their qualifications were, but I was assured the mystery orb was perfectly safe.

Neighbors and friends soon weighed in, offering various theories. My instant favorite was that it had fallen off John Frémont's wagon, ammunition for the infamous howitzer that he, ignoring his superiors, controversially dragged for miles and months around the West to ward off enemies real and imagined.

According to information available online about Frémont's cannon, the dimensions of this sphere, taking into account a few millimeters of rust, are, well, close. I confess I have not had the ball examined by a historian, and Frémont's path through central Oregon doesn't favor this theory, unless he stopped to picnic by the Deschutes River, which he did, and a cannonball just happened to roll off the wagon, which it could have. Whatever the truth about this globe, I like to believe there are no accidents in life. The discovery of it led me to learn more about John Frémont and his remarkable wife, Jessie Benton Frémont.

Having explored the Rocky Mountains in 1842, the next year John Frémont set off on his second mapping expedition of the West, from The Dalles, Oregon, to Sacramento, California. Originally billed as a nine-month journey, he decided to detour through the Great Basin of Oregon, Oregon Desert Trail country, and then head to California, traversing the Sierra Nevada. The detour extended the trip by four months and subjected the members of the expedition to terrible hardships, including those atop Winter Ridge. Thanks to Jessie's writing skills (for which she never received any credit), his report was imbued with his love of open spaces that promote "freedom of eye and thought." The six-hundred-page document presented to Congress in 1845 included maps, sketches, and practical advice for settlers, proving to be a guide for those who followed.

Had it not been for an old water line and the discovery of a heavy, rusty ball, I might never have learned about John and Jessie Frémont. And how curious that, thirty years later, I wound up living underneath the brow of Winter Ridge. Rather than accidents, in my experience these are the invitations that wait on the sidelines of every trail and every path we're on.

Another of many examples from my own experiences of this kind of sequential serendipity was when walking the Camino de Santiago in Spain. Following in the footsteps of thousands of pilgrims, penitents, and seekers over the centuries, I was in search of answers to "What's next?" A month spent walking alongside others with their separate sets of petitions, my worldly needs contained in a small backpack, seemed the right prescription for getting at answers.

But the list of life questions I was certain I'd resolve while walking the Way was quickly supplanted by what the camino had in mind, including, as it turns out, what I'd write next. When I got back to Oregon and was sorting through brochures and mementos of the trip, I stumbled upon a map of the ten camino routes that converge in Santiago. What jumped out at me, looking at that small map, was the stick-figure outline of a woman leaping. In that moment Camino Woman was born in my imagination and she wouldn't let me go. She insisted on being written. The result of this creative epiphany was a verse novel published in 2014 that I subsequently converted into a libretto. It premiered as an opera in 2016. These happy chances and what they produced were cousins to the discovery of the rusty metal ball and all that resulted from that unearthing. Now serving as a doorstop in my house, each time I walk by it I am reminded to stay awake, to look out of the corner of my eye.

In *The Songlines*, Bruce Chatwin writes of a "labyrinth of invisible pathways which meander all over Australia and are known as 'Dreaming Tracks' or 'Songlines.'" He explains that Aboriginal creation myths describe legendary beings who wandered over the continent in Dreamtime, before life, singing out the name of everything that crossed their path—birds, animals, plants, rocks, water holes—and thus "singing" the world into existence. Each ancestor was thought to have scattered a trail of words and musical notes along his footprints. Those coming later, if they knew the song, could always find their way. According to the Songlines, before we can exist in what we call reality, we have to be sung into existence, that is, to exist we first have to be perceived. What is tantalizing is that this creation myth resembles the various Native American creation myths, resembles the Bible's creation of living things, and parallels Buddhism's perception of reality.

It is on this section of the trail, especially, where it's possible to glimpse, for a split second, that just behind the conscious and visible order of things there lies a shared world of abstract, peripheral, metaphorical, and spiritual reality that appears from time to time in the everyday world. It lives in the space between breaths. Between waking and sleeping. Between ending and beginning again. Between one footstep and the next. To paraphrase Paul Tillich in his book *The New Being*, be "grasped by a power that is greater than we are, a power that shakes us and turns us, and transforms us and heals us." As you walk these trails and make your own, you'll glimpse the infinite inside the world as well as outside it.

But what exactly is a trail? If a songline, then what are the words to the ODT? What are the lyrics of the songlines of early inhabitants whose paths we are crossing? Can we hear them? Am I on "my" trail? Are you on yours? Is that even the question? It seems not. Instead, with your basket of words, sing something good into existence.

Trails have never been purely utilitarian. They have always led to sources of food, water, heat, materials for creating shelter. They still do. But they have also been for something else as well, for pausing, pondering, and reflection. What the pausing and pondering do for perspective is as important as where the trail leads, keeping us open to the invitations and opportunities dancing in our peripheral vision, to an affection for uncertainty.

✦

Before accepting the post of executive director, as a writer I enjoyed the gift of a number of residencies at PLAYA. I had been exploring the Oregon Desert Trail, but the idea for this book grabbed me, became something I couldn't not do, during a stint at PLAYA. I place some of the inspirational blame at the feet of photographer Terri Warpinski of Eugene, Oregon, who was there when I was along with other resident artists luxuriating in uninterrupted time to create. She used her residency to complete a book of her images, to expand her portfolio of desert photographs, but also, every day—either to keep her sanity or because she had lost it while so immersed in her art—she would walk out into the vacant stare of the playa to add a few more black volcanic rocks to a straight line she was drawing across the gray, brittle, cracked surface of the dried lake bed.

Those of us artists in residence paid it little mind at first, but then in conversations over dinner this trail of rocks began to engage us. When I first noticed it, I assumed it was a fence line. That didn't make sense. Were those footprints? Eventually we learned it was Terri's creation. Did the line of rocks go to the far shore? Why was Terri doing it? How did she get the rocks there? These musings in and of themselves expanded our relationship with the playa whether we set foot on it or not. A few residents, giving in to their curiosity, walked the Morse code of it as far as it went then turned around and came back; still others kept going to assess the remaining distance to the far shore, which, mirage-like, always remained a mile or so out of reach.

That's what I did. I walked past where Terri's trail of rocks ended. I soon found myself running as though afraid, as though I wanted to get it over with, wanted to get to the other shore and then return to the security of the marked trail that had disappeared from view behind me. The absence of the rocks was somehow unsettling to me. No guide. On my own. Unmarked, uncharted, wild out there in the middle of that vast, inscrutable playa. Life's trail.

Maybe a trail is a way of challenging death. Start at the beginning of something, go to the end—and then, instead of stopping (dying), step off into an undefined else. What are each of us leaving and going toward? Maybe too much of what we do in life is taken up by trying to find the right trail, to resolve ourselves and our lives into a discernable pattern and direction and always in denial about the fact that the trail, as we perceive it, has an end. Even better, make that trail one you don't have to bushwhack, that is already charted. Most of us are happier with a trail than without one. The reassurance of knowing the remaining distance back to home base, of a known trail, makes us brave-ish. Most of us are happier when someone else is with us on that trail rather than all by ourselves. Most of us are happier with mediated wilderness, guided wilderness, the cruise-shipping of wilderness.

The real McCoy requires that we actually know about survival, finding our way, being without contact, being dirty and uncomfortable for more than a few nights, maybe even lost. Maybe the whole point is to get lost from time to time. Maybe "I found the trail!"—the call you shout back to your hiking companion when you have both lost track—couldn't possibly feel so good without first getting lost.

Here's to the Oregon Desert Trail. It gives you ample room and opportunity to feel lost because it doesn't hold your hand. You map your own way. You swim or sink in the sagebrush ocean. You have the freedom to roam, to call your path your own. When you started in the Oregon Badlands in Bend many day hikers were outfitted in enough gear to survive Everest but had little occasion to use most of it. Thru-hikers will have put their gear and themselves to the test.

By now, elated though exhausted, you emerge from the south end of Summer Lake. You're finally off the uneven, pocked desert ground and on a dirt road leading to Paisley for restocking after being transported by winds, amazing vistas, and sheer determination. Maybe you'll stop for a soak in the Summer Lake Hot Springs and get cleaned up before heading to Paisley for a night on a real bed after an organic burger at the Pioneer Saloon. How good that will feel. How tired your bones are.

A friend once told me about flying his private plane from Bend to Portland over Mount Hood on a pristine day. He spied a climber

laboring up the final, treacherous distance to the summit and calcu-
lated the alpinist had to have gotten up at 3:00 a.m. or so to make the
eleven-thousand-foot ascent by that time in the morning. Impressive.
He circled back, flew close above the climber, and dipped a wing in
a congratulatory salute. In return, the climber gestured emphatically
with his middle finger. *How dare you crash my accomplishment unin-
vited! How dare you insert the rude presence of your plane in this pristine,
solo, exquisite moment of mine!*

As you flank Highway 31 on your way to Paisley, pickup trucks
speeding by, making light of distance and effort, just wave them on
and sing the world, your world, into being.

EIGHT

Rurally Underserved

I 'M AN NBA fan. Go figure. Those who know me would never have guessed. I attribute it to the fact that when my late husband and I first moved to our remote high-desert ranch north of Brothers, Oregon, the Blazers had recently won their 1977 NBA title. Blazer-mania. The whole state seemed like a small town, one community cheering for one same thing. One shared focus, one hope, one real-ized victory. Over the intervening years I've sat courtside at Blazer games, shouted "Jerome, take me home!" in the '90s, chanted "The ref beats his wife" with the best of them, tried to take life's hits the way Robin Lopez took the more literal kind under the basket, cheered the Lillard-McCollum duo, enjoyed a VIP dinner with the team, but I have to say the single most entertaining basketball game I ever saw was at the Paisley School gym.

Paisley is a sports-friendly and, especially, basketball-friendly town. Balls are left in the paved blacktop community playground, the nets albeit a bit frayed, the hoops a bit rusted. After a meal at the

Pioneer, you can play a quick round of H-O-R-S-E before hitting the road, a rural digestif.

The town's high school gym is so small you're inadvertently on court when you sit courtside on the wooden bleachers. As the game unfolds, in sync with the stampede of players up and down the court, spectators tuck or bend their legs to stay out of the way, a kind of seated chorus line. The game I attended was against Christian Academy of Bend, a fellow 1A team (the classification based on school population, with 1A being the very lowest). The score was tied. Double overtime. As a last-ditch effort, Paisley brought in a free thrower who had not been on the court thus far into the game. A slight, wiry kid from Montenegro, this was his first season of basketball. For that matter, this was his first season in America: a year at Paisley School. He was slight, small, with a corona of wild black hair. He walked to the line. Shrugged a couple of times and took a deep breath. To tie and keep the overtime going he had to make one basket. To end the overtime and win the game, he had to make two. He sank them both. Everyone, including the opposing team, was dumbfounded. As was he. After a momentary stunned silence, everyone leapt to their feet, cheering the newly minted hero.

Paisley is a good resupply point for ODT thru-hikers. After Summer Lake, having temporarily forgotten how dry the desert can be, you have a new lease on life. Plus there's the well-stocked Paisley Mercantile (gun rights signs in the window notwithstanding), a restaurant, a library with internet, a post office, a drive-through coffee stand, and the nearby Summer Lake Hot Springs—all a trekker could want or need. Paisley is in Lake County—a county that has no stoplights and more roadless area than anywhere in the United States outside of Alaska. Part of the Oregon Outback, the county has as many square miles as people: eight thousand. After Lakeview, population twenty-three hundred, and Christmas Valley, population thirteen hundred, Paisley is the county's third-largest community with a population of two hundred. Paisley has its own school district, administrative offices, and classrooms housed in one distinguished old stone building. The school serves approximately ninety students K–12, the number rising and falling depending on which ranch hands and ranch owners have school-age children on a given year, how many graduated the previous spring, or which Paisley enterprise has expanded or shuttered. In Lake County there's no excuse for not attending college after graduation, thanks to Lakeview's educational trust fund established in the 1900s by Dr. Bernard Daly. Along with a number of other scholarships sponsored by businesses and ranchers, it finances a college education for Lake County students who complete all four years of high school in the county. Daly was born in Ireland and immigrated to the United States. After serving in the army, he moved to Lake County in 1887. In 1922, he gave his first scholarship to a young woman who had been working for him. She went on to become a doctor, like Daly. That set the stage, a competition of sorts, for ranchers, business people, and others to develop their own scholarships. Paisley students, along with others in Lake County, take full advantage. That's the good news.

The not-good news is that the Paisley School is constantly dodging the threat of closure. If its enrollment drops too low, it doesn't qualify for state support and can't pay staff. To prevent that possibility, in 1995 the school board decided to create an international dormitory for high school students. The program attracts about twelve students a year from all over the world, about a third of the upperclassmen. Former Paisley School District superintendent William Wurtz put it bluntly:

"If we don't have kids in our dorm, we don't have a high school." That ringer from Montenegro who sealed the basketball victory for Paisley, he was one of the international students.

They think they are coming to the America of their imaginations: urban, hip, Las Vegas or Los Angeles or New York, not "the big empty," as Lake County is sometimes referred to. I would love to capture on video their arrival and the expressions of shock when they see the dorm, the town, the vast landscape. And then, in a few weeks, return to document the signs of them starting to love the community, its people, and vice versa.

In addition to the basketball game, I have experienced other "bests" thanks to Paisley School and its unusual student population. Among them was the school's production of *Mary Poppins*. It involved pretty much the entire student body and was produced under the skilled direction of the Paisley School drama instructor, Kris Norris. The lead role of Jack was played by a Ukrainian student for whom English was a distant second language, making it a challenge to speak, never mind sing, in a Cockney accent. But the confidence and enthusiasm he and every student, international and otherwise, put into the effort was absolutely showstopping. While at Paisley School, the international students are encouraged to take part in everything—sports, high school plays, student council, debate team, wood shop and art class—and deejay as well as attend school dances. And then there are the community dinners.

In 2015 John Steffes and Rebecca Steele, an intrepid young couple from Portland, purchased the Pioneer Saloon. It is one of the oldest pubs in Oregon, having started serving drinks in 1883. The couple collaborated with Paisley School to raise money for school field trips whereby the international students, one per month when school is in session, take over the Pioneer Saloon's kitchen and prepare a traditional meal from their country. They print information about their homeland on paper placemats—including a reproduction of their national flag and a few statistics like population, religions, type of government—followed by a description of the meal they will serve. The simple act of breaking bread together at the Pioneer, young people serving the community, is the ultimate friendly persuasion, gently changing the diners' opinions about people of color and of different religious persuasions. It's powerful in its simplicity, a model for healing divisions in this so-called United States and the world.

Mind you, this is a county and community that is 90 percent white and politically red. The common denominator among all residents is hard work. Given the vagaries of cattle prices, fuel prices, the weather's effect on hay crops and so on, income is middle to low even for those families who own their large ranches free and clear. Only the large corporate ranches have a significant margin for financial error. Paisley has Methodist, Jehovah's Witness, and Catholic churches. I think it's fair to assume people of color or with different religious beliefs don't generally fit in the worldview held by most in and around Paisley. But in addition to the friendly and persuasive effect of the presence of the international students, open-mindedness is being encouraged in other unanticipated ways that promote a more accepting outlook whether Paisley residents are happy about it or not. The Catholic Church has an increasingly difficult time recruiting priests to rural parishes, and in many cases Catholic churches, including those along the ODT, are led by priests from African countries, India, the Middle East, Mexico, or Central America. In Paisley, those who might harbor an attitude about people of color are not only being served a meal by people of color, they are confessing their sins to a person of color. As Michelle Obama says in her memoir *Becoming*, "It's harder to hate up close."

Less dramatically, the artists and scientists in residence at PLAYA, up the road from Paisley, also provide the small town's residents an opportunity to rethink their view of city folk. It's a two-way invitation, as PLAYA artists are given an opportunity to get to know the real rural deal. Based on lack of exposure, the polarizing tendency on the part of urbanites is to paint all small, rural communities the same political, educational, cultural, and philosophical color. Even to fear their inhabitants.

An obituary in the *Bend Bulletin* caught my attention. The regional language and culture reflected in the eulogy, the homespun expression of love and respect for an honest and true life, as close to a definition of *salt of the earth* as you can get. Gerald Albert Jerry George, the death notice established, died at age eighty-two at his high-desert home. He was born at his grandmother's house to Skinny and Dode. He served in the Korean War, then went to work as a log hauler. One of his bosses was named Bump. According to the obituary, "He loved going hunting with friends for the social part and not to shoot animals." He was "a beloved husband, grandfather, papa and da." His survivors include his wife, seven children, three adopted daughters, fifteen grandchildren, and "numerous great-grandchildren." "Other than the air force, Jerry lived and worked all his life in his beloved state of Oregon."

I didn't know Jerry but would have liked to. I don't know what his politics were, but this plainsong of a life well lived underscores the values of the people of rural America, the values of all principled people everywhere. We all fly the same colors. We are more the same than not. "It's not a matter of loving your enemies," said Father Gregory Boyle, founder of Homeboy Industries and the author of *Tattoos on the Heart*. "It's a matter of not having any."

In one form or another I have been involved with state arts commissions and arts nonprofits, primarily in literary arts, since moving West to ranch, first in Montana then in Oregon. In the high desert of central Oregon pretty much all communities are considered rural with the relatively recent exception of Bend. That designation is a definite help when applying for state and federal grants, as is the popular catchphrase "culturally underserved" in reference to the communities the proposed cultural program would benefit. The implication is that these communities are cultural wastelands and those in the cultured know are ready to act as missionaries, bringing the arts to the heathens. I don't suggest that in most cases the programs aren't a great thing. They are. Music and visual, performing, and literary arts programs find their way to rural community centers, libraries, and schools. Artists come and instruct for months at a time in schools that no longer have an arts or music curriculum. But the spirit in which funding is requested or programming is offered is what I question. Artists as taste- and culture-makers. Top down. The attitude is that the information they bring from the outside is the gospel, that the community in and of itself is clueless and has little to offer them. They had best heed the final line from Ursula Le Guin's poem "High Desert": *"here is another way to be."*

When I served in the Peace Corps it was clear that the benefit was equal if not greater for the volunteer than for the villages served. Volunteers learned about family, community, hard work, asking for and expecting less, and they gained some humility when it came to the wisdom of those they had come to proselytize. I personally experienced the same thing while ranching in Crook County, and more recently, residing in Lake County. A lot of practical lessons but also important life ones.

Dick Linford, founder of Echo River Trips and coauthor of *Half-way to Halfway and Other River Stories*, recalls a guest on a float trip on Oregon's beautiful Rogue River. One morning she emerged from her tent decked out in brand-new quick-wicking everything. She stretched, sipped her coffee while gazing at the roiling river, then turned to a guide packing up the raft for that day's adventure on the river and asked, dead serious, "Which way are we going today?" Many urban artists coming to PLAYA can't light a wood fire, don't know the difference between a cow and a heifer, a bull and a steer, what happens seasonally on a farm or ranch, what it takes to put meat on the table. But when they arrive, do they ever have opinions about cattle on rangeland or returning lands to their "natural" state, as though it were possible. The marketing of environmental and con-servation points of view has outpaced those who are working the land. There are valid points on both sides, but the disconnect between consuming, say, beef and protesting what it takes to produce it is impressive. Most of us used to have a relative who ranched or farmed that we would visit during the summer to help put up hay, feed the pigs and chickens, can fruit, milk cows. But now, no. Increasingly the agricultural economy is getting big-boxed. Rural communities and smaller agricultural concerns are struggling. And we all lose.

Adam Davis, the executive director of Oregon Humanities, facili-tated a conversation at the Paisley Community Center between the students of Ridgedale, an upscale high school in Portland, and the middle and high school students of Paisley. Adam's questions: One word to describe self. One word to describe how you define commu-nity, where is it for you, the place you feel comfortable. One word to describe a place that makes you feel uncomfortable. Paisley students' answers were generally positive, solid. Community was defined by the events surrounding, say, a branding when all the neighbors come and help or "punching" cows (which required translation for the students from Portland who pictured the young speaker literally delivering a left hook to the jaw of a recalcitrant cow). Uncomfortable was described as getting too far from home. Whereas the Paisley answers painted a social landscape that was nurturing and caring, the Portland students' answers trended toward one that felt as empty and lonely as the city kids perceived the Oregon Outback to be. It is exactly this nurturing that the international students come to appreciate, many from large cities and households where money is no object but perhaps the gift of a cohesive and supportive family and community is.

Did I hear this story in Paisley? I think so. In any case, a rural high-desert middle school took a field trip to the Oregon Museum of Science and Industry in Portland. They took their seats in the van-sized school bus for the five-hour drive, chatting excitedly all the way. At the museum they lined up with their teacher and chaperones, tickets in hand. Most of the young students were dressed in shirts, creased jeans that broke just so over the top of their cowboy boots, shiny belt buckles, and cowboy hats. Another school group, from Portland, filed in and lined up behind them. They displayed mixed plumage: caps on frontward or back, droopy or skin-tight pants, and T-shirts pledging allegiance to their school, various music groups, or sporting events. They wore knapsacks on their backs, had earbuds mainlining music into their ears, and cell phones in hand. One member of the city contingent stepped back to study the rural delegation's garb and mannerisms and felt compelled to ask: "What *are* you?" After a pause one of the Paisley middle schoolers stated matter-of-factly: "Cowboys. We're cowboys." Processing that response for a few seconds, the kid from the city turned to his peers and asked: "What are *we*?" Indeed. How would you answer that question about yourself, about your home culture?

It was after witnessing residents at PLAYA, hearing such stories as Dick Linford's, and listening to Adam Davis skillfully engage the students from Portland and Paisley that I realized that most of us nowadays are rurally underserved. At my accountant's office recently, I stood in the reception area next to a woman finalizing her taxes and the word *steer* was mentioned for some reason. What was a steer, one asked the other? A bull without horns, ventured one? I volunteered it was a castrated bull, nothing to do with horns. How about a cow versus a heifer? I asked. No idea, they said. I explained the difference: a heifer has never had a calf. Once she loses her bovine virginity, she's a cow. I then recited the refrain in my effort at country and western lyrics: "It's now or never, I ain't no heifer anymore." They identified.

So often as executive director at PLAYA, I encountered creative, risk-taking, brilliant artists who had zero idea of how to engage with or survive in a nonurban setting. It was then I decided to shift the emphasis in the grants I was writing on behalf of PLAYA to encourage the appreciation of what each had to offer the other. Culturally underserved might (and might not) apply to those in rural areas, but what is true is that the majority of us are most definitely rurally underserved.

Taylor and Becky Hyde, a ranching couple who live part-time in Paisley, know exactly what they are. I first met Becky as a young girl. Her family's ranch just north of Brothers, Oregon, bordered ours. The Hydes operate century ranches, with land holdings in the same family for that long. Those traveling on the Oregon Desert Trail pass these venerable ranches as they proceed up and out of Paisley, across to Plush, Adel, and on to the emerald gem of Hart Mountain.

Becky, her long arms flung wide to take in all the territory she describes, rightfully claims that "all of the high desert is my community." She is speaking figuratively, but she can legitimately make that claim in a literal sense. She and her husband own and operate ranches that take in portions of Crook, Deschutes, and Klamath Counties near the communities of Brothers, Chiloquin, and Beatty. They maintain a house in Paisley where their children, five of them, attend school. Two have graduated, three more to go. It's an unwieldy, rambling house half a block from school. Thanks to the previous owners' penchant for adding an extra room here, a back porch there, when I visited for the first time it wasn't obvious which of the doors was the front one. But the extra nooks and crannies have been repurposed to accommodate each child's hobbies and creativity. One room is set aside for the middle son's leatherwork with his collection of small, elegant tools lined up precisely on his worktable. Another functions as a gallery for his younger brother's artwork depicting fantastical landscapes and creatures. Coat hooks in an entry hall have been recruited for guitar cases, sports gear, chaps, spurs, and ropes and on the floor under the hooks, every manner of footwear from irrigation boots and cowboy boots to felts, track and basketball shoes, flip-flops. Bookshelves sag under all sorts of titles—how-tos to Shakespeare to range management.

Becky and her husband are ranching royalty in a way. She is the daughter of Doc and Connie Hatfield, who launched Oregon Country Natural Beef over thirty years ago, the first natural, grass-fed beef cooperative in Oregon. Doc was also credited with introducing the Alan Savory holistic range management practices to the high desert, which Savory, born in 1935, had perfected in Rhodesia. Doc Hatfield subscribed to the Savory system's ability to reverse the desertification of brittle grasslands by shortening the stay of cattle on any particular pasture, giving plant species time to recover before the herd cycled back around to graze the same area. Oregon State University representatives and foreign visitors, curious about the successes Doc achieved using the range management program, were frequent visitors to the Hatfield Ranch. Becky was weaned on the big-picture thinking that her parents embodied, and it shows.

Her husband, Taylor, grew up on the historic Yamsi Ranch in Chiloquin, Oregon, located on the Klamath Marsh and Williamson River, the ranch having been in his family since 1911. It's easy to run out of superlatives when trying to describe various places in Oregon's high desert, and this Williamson River valley ranch is one of them. The ranching management practices at the Yamsi are as holistic and progressive as they come. Despite the miles of driving, the mercurial weather, the impossible logistics, and the changing nature of the business of ranching, Taylor and Becky wouldn't dream of doing anything else with their lives. Avocation and vocation are the same to them. Both are armed with the powerful combination of excellent educations and the requisite get 'er done attitude that comes from growing up on a ranch. Need to know something while living one hundred miles from town? Figure out how to figure it out.

Taylor and Becky are engaged in water rights advocacy work and cattle and rangeland issues; they are members of boards and committees that touch on key concerns for ranchers everywhere. One century ranch owner in Paisley claims that larger family ranches are confronted with a new environmentally related lawsuit every six months or so. Corporate ranching neighbors like the ZX have company lawyers, but individually owned and operated ranches have mother cows to turn out, calves to brand and wean, fields to hay, bookkeeping to do, never mind families to raise and PTA meetings and basketball tournaments to attend. Stretched thin, they make an easy target. "I can't begin to explain what it takes today to make a living from the land," says Becky Hyde. "In addition to everything else, a rancher has to stay up-to-date about endangered species policies, including the sage grouse and wolves, fire management, state and federal water policies, BLM and Forest Service rules and regs, wilderness and monument proposals affecting grazing, and that's just for starters." Why do it? Like most ranchers she attributes it to "our deep love of soil, of land."

In addition to helping on his parents' ranches, Becky and Taylor's middle son Henry spends his summers wrangling for a neighboring Summer Lake ranch. He's up at dawn, on horseback all day pushing cattle up and over Diablo, into and up Cat Canyon, down into Sycan Marsh, over toward Hart Mountain. It's all he wants to do. For him it is truly second nature to strap on his leather chaps, grab his rope, stuff his saddlebag with a waterproof poncho and a sandwich he threw together the night before. Does he have any idea what an endangered species he, his family's way of life, and the cowboy culture is?

Jack, Henry's older brother, got an Oregon Ford Foundation scholarship to attend Lewis and Clark College when he graduated from Paisley School in 2018. As part of his college application, he wrote an essay describing his ambition to start a rural banking system to promote and support the efforts of rural families so they could stay in the small communities they loved rather than be forced to leave to look for work elsewhere due to shrinking economies and constricting land-use policies. In his essay he advocated for a positive platform for rural voices and described the signs of the terrible need: businesses for sale, empty storefronts, corporate ranches, unemployment, drug use. For Henry's sake, for the sake of the towns like Paisley, Plush, Adel, and Fields located along the Oregon Desert Trail, and the many others like them across the United States, hopefully Jack makes good on his ambition. Because if Jack doesn't succeed, there's going to be serious collateral damage, and not only the real-time loss of these communities.

NINE

Losing Language

L EAVING PAISLEY, THE Oregon Desert Trail parallels the Chewaucan River and climbs up into ponderosa-studded canyons
and natural meadows. You're likely to see evidence of mountain lion
quickly followed by the slightly chilling realization as to why the area
of rock outcroppings you're walking through is called Cat Canyon.
If you're like me, you'll nervously try to recall what to do should you
encounter the large cat. Look bigger? Smaller? Or was that if you
ran into a bear? Make eye contact? Don't? Run? Stand still? Climb
a tree? Phone home? The other less-than-consoling advice I got
about cougars is: "Don't worry. They only attack from behind so
you'll never know what happened." What *is* consoling is that this
beautiful cat still prowls a territory it has prowled for centuries. But
the mysterious and elegant Paiute word for them, *tooonugwetsedu*, is
rarely encountered.

A group of western writers, scientists, and environmentalists
assemble biennially at the Andrews Experimental Forest on the

McKenzie River. It's one of many symposia and gatherings organized by the Spring Creek Project of Oregon State University, which
has the goal of bringing together "the practical wisdom of the environmental sciences, the clarity of philosophical analysis, and the creative, expressive power of the written word to find new ways to
understand and re-imagine our relation to the natural world." Before
she died, Ursula Le Guin frequently attended. John Calderazzo,
Charles Goodrich, Jerry Martien, Kathleen Dean Moore, David Oates,
Carolyn Servid, Kim Stafford, and Fred Swanson are among the
regulars coming from Arcata, Anchorage, Fort Collins, and beyond
for a weekend of inspiration and restoration.

In a morning workshop at the 2018 gathering, Oregon poet
laureate Kim Stafford offered this quote from author Robert Macfarlane: "Once a landscape goes undescribed and therefore unregarded, it becomes more vulnerable to unwise use or improper
action." Macfarlane nails what happens to nature, to landscape if
unregarded, all the magnificent this, that, and those places; the two-,
four-, and eight-legged; the invertebrate and vertebrate, the crawlers
and fliers. By extension, it also explains what happens to groups of
people who feel disenfranchised and unwitnessed and why unwise
actions follow. Or language. Beautiful language left to languish.
Everything suffers if not regarded, becomes vulnerable to unwise
use, improper action, neglect, or abandonment. Macfarlane rein-
forced this in his response to the number of words associated with
nature that were eliminated from the 2012 revision of the *Oxford
Junior Dictionary*: "We do not care for what we do not know, and on
the whole we do not know what we cannot name. Do we want an
alphabet for children that begins 'A is for Acorn, B is for Buttercup,
C is for Conker'; or one that begins 'A is for Attachment, B is for Block-
Graph, C is for Chatroom'?"

In the natural world, evidence of the effects of our unnaming is everywhere. It is estimated by scientists that two hundred species of plants, insects, birds, and mammals become extinct every twenty-four hours thanks to unwise use of land, of air, of water. This is one thousand times the natural rate of five becoming extinct per year. The speculation is that we are hurtling toward what has been dubbed the sixth extinction in Elizabeth Kolbert's book of the same name. The last one, sixty-five million years ago, wiped out the dinosaurs. An asteroid was the cause. This time, we've only ourselves to blame.

In this high desert, the habitat for the spotted frog and sage grouse are deemed threatened; burrowing owls are a species of concern. The names of endangered high-desert plants are painful to read, given the color and variety in their names alone, never mind the disappearing flourish of the plants themselves: Applegate's milk-vetch, large-flowered woolly meadowfoam, McFarlane's four o'clock, rough popcorn flower, Malheur wire-lettuce.

According to John Martin, Walla Walla, Washington, poet and acute observer of such things, in 2017 the barn swallows up and left Summer Lake on August 3. They left their mud daub village under the eaves of the barn. All of them. The night before, they were there, entertaining with their midair acrobatics and ballet. The next night, the aerial stage was empty. So sudden. As though someone had done something to piss them off. "We're outta here! We'll go somewhere else. Enough with this new season called 'Smoke,' the humans who knock down our nests, the savage outdoor cats (they kill 3.7 billion birds a year and 20.7 billion mammals in the United States alone), the fertilizer on the ground, plastics in the water, the wind turbines along migratory paths, the loss of habitat."

But they came back the next spring. Despite recent reports that bird populations have fallen by 30 percent since 1970, where else can they go that isn't also under siege? Is it instinct? Or is it the avian expression of forgiveness, albeit misplaced, of the ones with the biggest brains. Animals and birds are migrating in search of places where they can survive. These wildlife refugees are striking out across unknown territory, struggling to get there against all odds, traversing borders and barricades. What does this remind you of? What walls are humans inadvertently or unnecessarily erecting?

As for flora in the high desert, it's all uphill from here. High-desert species are doing what species everywhere are doing in response to warming temperatures. They are scaling mountains, or trying to get to an altitude with the temperature ranges they need to flourish. When you're going through hell, keep going. Across from the Oregon Desert Trail along Summer Lake, plants are slowly, seasonally clambering up the seven-thousand-foot Winter Ridge to find new homes. In Brazil an effort is underway on industrial-sized farms to intersperse small sections of native plants where migrating flora that survived the fires of 2019 can "rest" on the way to higher elevations. Picture flora ladders, like fish ladders, so species can make their way across vast agricultural monocultures. I imagine a futuristic fable, a sad one, about the abandonment of earth and the creation of new constellations in the night sky, as all the flora and fauna are forced to higher and higher climes, eventually taking their place among the stars.

This precipitous loss of the plant and animal is tragic, frightening. But as tragic to me is the loss of the sound of the wind through a stand of native wild rye, the fragrance of the desert lily in bloom, the mating call of the sage grouse, the nervous giggle of the coyote, the whinny of the wild Kiger mustang.

And what of the loss of words? Think of the world inhabited by people for whom black is *toohoo*, *toha* is white. *Ese* is gray, *ont* is brown. *Atsa* is red. Green and blue are both *poohe*. Sun is *taba*, moon is *muha*, water is *baa'a*, bald eagle is *ggwe'na'a*, field mouse is *poongatse*. The Paiute world. Isn't the diminishment of cultural habitat and the resulting endangerment of the languages of Native American nations, of vaqueros and cowboys, as tragic as the loss of the soft, conversational *chuk-chuk* of the sage grouse or plaintive howl of the wolf? Thankfully valiant efforts are underway to protect and preserve the languages of both the two- and four-leggeds. They map where we've come from and provide a cautionary tale as to where we're headed.

As you head out of Paisley you could easily cross paths with Taylor and Becky's teenage son Henry and other buckaroos (from the Spanish *vaquero*) moving cattle out of the high forest, snapping their lariats (*las reatas*) against their legs, clicking and hooting, encouraging the herd along with a form of cowboy scat singing: *hut, hut, hiya, sshhh, sshh, hey-up, hey-up*! Nonsense syllables, wordless vocables used over decades by cowboys from Mexico to Canada to urge cattle down the trail. Henry might tell fellow riders about the rock jacks he built, the cavvy of horses he gathered that morning, boast about his success roping Corrientes (a breed of cattle brought to the Americas by the Spanish as early as 1493) at the local jackpot team roping, missing his dally when trying to rope and doctor a leppy (orphaned) bull calf in the open meadow, while the healthy ones hightailed it, tails crooked in the air. He might admire the conchas on his fellow riders' bit, how glad he was for his protective tapaderos and chaps riding through the dense mountain mahogany. He might admire a cowboy's toughness—"harder than a picnic egg"—or advise his friend riding a snuffy (counterfeit colt), to "keep a deep seat and a loose rein". Older cowboys on the drive might admonish "Make a hand!" or "Cowboy up!" Wranglers might use what is called a domesticated "prather" horse—also called a "Judas" horse—to lead wild horses into a corral. The wild ones are referred to as broomtails, fuzztails, or mustangs. The language of the cowboy culture is effortlessly, unselfconsciously woven into every sentence.

The riders trade stories only ranching could spawn, like the one about the cowpoke who boasted he could drive all day long in his pickup and never get to the southern boundary of his ranch. The other cowboy, unimpressed, replied: "I used to have a truck like that too. Not worth a damn." One cowhand might counsel the other to lay a rope in a circle around his bedroll when sleeping on the desert floor. No snake will cross . . . too bristly. "Jesus Christ on Cow Creek" was the least of the invectives used when a rancher discovered that a well-meaning thru-hiker had opened a gate and let his yearling calves out, the ones he had just moved to a new pasture. The hiker, not knowing the curious-about-everything, looking-for-trouble behavior of yearlings, famous for their middle school mentality, apparently thought they were in distress as they worried the fence line at a trot, exploring their new digs.

✦

And the timber industry? Whatever you think of the practice of timber harvest, the language and culture has vanished. No more sounds of cork boots on the sidewalks of timber towns. No more music of the muscular language and lives led by the men and their families who followed the trees. The story could as easily apply to the small mill at Paisley or the mills in Lakeview as it does to all the shuttered mills and mill towns throughout the Northwest. For Bend's loggers and millworkers, the nightmare came true starting on September 9, 1993. A "Memo to Employees" was circulated at Bend's Crown Pacific large-log mill announcing that the last large log would be processed through the mill that day at noon, signaling the final closure of that portion of mill operations. The informal plan was to allow each station operator the opportunity to perform his task one last time—loader, trimmer, debarker, scaler, sawyer, edger, filer, green chain, stacker, and planer. It is not clear whether mill management realized how important this impromptu ceremony would prove to be. Western corporate culture isn't known for recognizing the need for rituals— to celebrate beginnings, to give thanks, to grieve endings. Likewise, millworkers and loggers aren't credited for placing much stock in such events. And anyway, who would have thought this day would ever come?

After all, since 1915 lumber mills had defined Bend's skyline: towering smokestacks, massive wooden basilicas, wigwam burners, and railroad transoms. The timber industry provided the economic blood that gave life to the young town, attracting scores of workers from the Midwest—family man and outdoorsman, adventurer and artisan—to fell trees or process logs. Work in the woods and in the mills was a way of life that boasted its own language, dress, and customs and had put bread on the table of generations of central Oregonians.

In 1984 the City of Bend requested that the mill stop sounding the shift whistle, due to the numbers of complaints from white-collar newcomers to the growing community. When the whistle went mute, little did anyone realize what that silence forebodes. This was well before the spotted owl was a subject of household debate; before Earth First activists sank shards of metal into tree trunks to intentionally cause injury, or even death, to the logger whose saw struck the rogue metal; before people were camped in treetops, a human sacrifice to the preservation of a tree.

But sure enough, nine years later in the fall of 1993, Crown Pacific was forced to announce the closure of the large-log portion of the Bend mill. It seemed every day that year a mill closed somewhere in Oregon, economically and emotionally crippling entire communities overnight. In Bend, local workers and loggers alike wanted to believe that at least the small-mill portion of the Bend operation would continue to run. But anyone who took the time could see that the supply of raw material, regardless of the stump diameter, was dwindling due to stricter and stricter enforcement of cutting regulations, and that environmental victories had resulted in the prohibition of logging across enormous tracts of federal forest throughout the region. The small mill would close four months later.

The day the last large log was milled was almost disrespectful in its sunny, crisp, carefree giddiness, as days in that high-desert community are at that time of year. The gigantic, yellow front-end loader, gripping the enormous girth of the ponderosa in its talons, waddled on its massive cat tracks toward the belt that would receive the log and start it on its journey through the mill. Men in work boots, T-shirts, and overalls lined the ramp that skirted the belt, watching in respectful silence. The log crashed mightily off the loader into the cradle of the conveyor. The gears were thrust into forward, the wheels and cogs reluctantly starting to turn, screeching and wailing in protest as if they knew.

The log was forced through the trimmer and debarker, emerging white and pure, its round promise coming to a stop at the entrance to the dark interior of the mill. The conveyor belt was abruptly shut down, whining to a halt. Then, in startling silence, uninterrupted, not even by a cough or shuffle of feet, eighty-eight-year-old former forester Hans Milius stepped up to scale the log. In his hand he held a long wooden measuring device with a sharp hook on one end that was designed to grab the outside perimeter of the log. As the acknowledged elder and the barker of the log's last rites, he solemnly and deliberately called out the log's dimensions. He then passed the measuring stick, like a runner in a slow-motion relay, to another and then another, each younger than the previous, so that anyone who had ever done this job could have his final turn, confirming, as Hans had, that this was a big, beautiful, and generous pine, whose bounty would raise many a roof in and around the whole of the Northwest.

Just as suddenly the belt was started up again, and this time the head sawyers took turns slicing the log into boards. The first one stepped into the glassine-covered booth that looked like the control cab of a Ferris wheel. He took pains to carefully hone the outside of the boards to straight dimensions, swiveling on the chair, deftly wielding the gears, as the log rocked dumbly back and forth, more finely tuned with each pass. And then, as though choreographed in advance, the next sawyer, and then another, wordlessly stepped in behind, taking a last turn at his task that had for years meant clothes for the kids, a new ski boat, a pickup truck, the dishes the wife wanted, the La-Z-Boy, a VCR, tuition for the first in the family to attend college, or money for Saturday nights at the show.

Working in a small garret above were the band saw filers. The thirty-foot-long steel saw below them spun faster than the speed of sight, its offset metallic teeth gnawing furiously and surgically through the center of the log. Replacement blades lie in wait, loose and languid on the floor of the dimly lit workspace. The specialized skill of the band saw filer determined the kerf, or width, of the saw cut. The wider, the more waste. Every filer prided himself on his own technique for producing no kerf. Like everyone who worked the mills, he knew there was no place for waste in this profession. Tuned, the freshly sharpened saw was fed to the sawyer through a hole in the floor of the attic hideaway, then lifted on to the feeder belt and secured into position. At the flick of the switch the saw leapt back to lethal life, cutting the log cleanly in half again.

At each station the log's significance increased in proportion to its diminishing size. Each time the gears were stopped, the real and symbolic significance of the mighty partnership of man and machine was framed by the silence, as immense as the interior of the mill itself.

The log now lay cut into smooth, even, white planks and stacked, ready for the dry kiln. The machines and cranes and saws and belts in the large-log mill on the banks of the Deschutes River were silenced forever. But the men assembled there, with no prompting, engaged in a last act of defiance against the course of history. As one, they moved toward the pulley that triggered the shift whistle. They pulled hard on the rope, and the whistle sounded long and sang loud of the machines and the men who operated them, offered shrill thanks to the evergreen forests that surrounded them. When finally it stopped sounding, the men let out a gruff, uneven cheer, tripped up by their emotions, and wordlessly walked out of the building, their tin lunch pails and hard hats in hand. Three-fourths of Oregon's lumber mills would close between 1980 and 2010.

Walking the ODT, thru-hikers will be flummoxed by cairns perched on hilltops or mountaintops, or a random run of wall built out of volcanic tuff pitching headlong down a steep, sagebrush-studded face, starting at nothing that feels like a beginning, stopping at nothing that feels like an end. Who built them and why? Since the late 1880s Basque sheepherders have been ranching throughout the Great Basin, including in the communities of Lakeview and Jordan Valley, both stopping points on the ODT. Those mysterious cairns? Directional markers. And the walls were used to deflect sheep and cattle as they were herded across this big country. Nevada author and poet Carolyn Dufurrena recalls a week spent in Elko, listening to the rhythms and difficult syllables of Euskera, the language of the Basque people, as part of the celebration of Basques and Buckaroos at an annual National Cowboy Poetry Gathering. Three young women, champion *bertsolaris* (improvisational singers) had traveled from Spain to demonstrate a cultural tradition they shared with their Nevada cousins. One, Maialen Lujanbo, was the first woman to have been crowned the national champion in Spain. "They sang back and forth," Dufurrena wrote in her blog, "pairing improvisational rhymes with traditional melodies."

On her way back from the gathering, she mused about the Basque tendency to remain: "Basques were right where they are now in Spain at the end of the last Glacial Age. Twelve-thousand-year-old Basque ancestors exhumed from the soft limestone cave of Santimamine in Gipuzkoa have the same DNA as the folk who live in the nearby village."

In the late nineteenth century, Basques fled to the United States. Many settled in the Great Basin and brought their staying power and strong linguistic and cultural traditions with them. We have Basques to thank for chorizo sausage, for *solomo* (pork loin cooked with sweet red peppers), for pelota (a mix of handball and racquetball; there's a court near the ODT's route in Jordan Valley), and peasant dances performed in Basque communities today. By 1910 Basque immigrants had spread into all the open-range areas of the West. But established cattle ranchers resented the presence of the itinerant Basque sheepherders and advocated for laws denying grazing to aliens and herders—specifically targeting the Basques. The Taylor Grazing Act placed almost all remaining public rangeland under federal control. With the act's grazing restrictions, itinerant herding was effectively ended and, coming at the height of the Great Depression, it caused severe economic hardship to the Basque community. Ironically, due to labor shortages, during World War II the lack of sheepherders resulted in federal legislation inviting sheepherders from Basque country in Spain back to the American West and prompted the arrival of a new wave of immigrants starting in the 1940s and continuing through the 1970s. They put down roots from Reno to Boise, Alturas, California, to Buffalo, Wyoming. The region has been referred to as the "Basque States of America." Says Dufurrena, "If history is to judge, [they] will be here for millennia to come. After all, it's in their DNA to remain and to preserve their culture." One of several cultural programs in the region is Boiseko Ikastola, a Basque language immersion preschool in Boise, Idaho—the only one of its kind in the United States. "*Non dago hiru?*" the children are asked. They point to the number three displayed on the classroom wall. "*Non dagu sei?*" They think for a moment and then single out the number six.

The word *triage*, from the French *tier*, "to separate out," comes to mind as policies and people play God in determining which animals, plants, peoples, cultures, and languages to save and which to sacrifice. The wolf has been defined as a beneficial species, its reintroduction in Yellowstone National Park, for example, positively affecting many aspects of the environment. Certain sharks are apex predators— having no aggressor—and worthy of protection because they can keep other less desirable species in check. What colors of the rainbow are we humans willing to live without? Inside our communities, our condos, our capitols, our castles, who among us are the beneficial species? The cover of William Catton's book *Overshoot: The Ecological Basis of Revolutionary Change* puts it bluntly:

CARRYING CAPACITY: maximum permanently supportable load.
CORNUCOPIAN MYTH: euphoric belief in limitless resources.
DRAWDOWN: stealing resources from the future.
CARGOISM: delusion that technology will always save us from
OVERSHOOT: growth beyond an area's carrying capacity, leading to
CRASH: die-off.

I would add: growth beyond a species' or a culture's capacity, leading to die-off. My optimism fails me here. With cloning and artificial intelligence on the horizon, perhaps all this is moot.

✦

Paisley hosts an annual cowboy poetry reading, a fundraiser for the "cowboy emergency fund" to help ranch hands who get injured and have no health insurance. It has prompted a lot of jokes, such as warning against "squatting with your spurs on." I first interpreted it as helping cowboys find their way through the grief that would accompany the loss of a way of life they loved and depended on for their livelihood and identity. The ballad-like cowboy poems are celebrations of a way of life but are also the cowboy version of the blues, odes to something that might be slipping through their fingers. Cowboys and ranchers can smell it. Like a storm brewing. For many human "species" as well as plant and animal, this trail feels like a long goodbye.

EAST BASIN AND RANGE

It comes down to feeling joy—an emotion I think is sadden-
ingly hard to come by. Everyone's gotta find their own way
to it. I think thru hiking has an advantage in that there is
a new surprise every day, there is a good deal of awe, there
is endorphins and exercise, there is meeting new people, and
there is a lot of time to think.

THRU-HIKER DANNY "CARIBOU" ARCHIBALD

TEN

That Cow Smiled at Me

I STOOD IN LINE at the US Bank in Lakeview, an optional "big city" detour for trekkers on the trail. On that Friday, payday, ten people were waiting ahead of me. The two tellers were going as fast as they could. The bank managers at their desks were also busy with customers. In Lakeview, waiting in line at the bank was not an aggravation; it was a social occasion. Everyone knew one another. I was the exception. Despite some polite nods of heads, tips of hats in my direction, I was a stranger. The conversations around me were seasonal, about place, family, and culture. "You turned out yet?" "Haying?" "How many cuttings ya thinkin'?" "How's the water?" "Find the extra help you needed?" One of those waiting in line was a trim young man wearing a black Gambler-style cowboy hat, sideburns down to his jawline, a trophy belt buckle picturing a cowboy, his rope like a halo over his head, chasing down a calf. "You still up there in Adel?" "Yessir. I am. Gettin' on ten horses a day so they're ready for the sale."

That this buckaroo had the opportunity to use time-honored skills breaking horses was not because he worked on a sprawling ranch that required a lot of horses. No. These traditions were preserved as the result of a well-intended program that, in my opinion, was dead on arrival. The "sale" the young cowboy in the bank was referring to was the first Beatys Butte Mustang Adoption Event.

Ten saddle-started, so-called wild horses, available for adoption would be auctioned, according to the posters around town. The event would be held at a new horse-training facility in Adel. If you skip the detour into Lakeview, the ODT heads east in that direction, essentially following the Fremont National Recreation Trail to Abert Rim, a massive fault scarp that abruptly rises twenty-five hundred feet above Lake Abert, Oregon's most saline lake. Gaining more altitude as the trail proceeds east toward Plush, hikers can take in the breathtaking panorama of Lake Abert to the north, Hart Mountain to the east, the Warner Mountains to the south, and the Chewaucan Valley and Paisley to the west.

Adel has a brand-spanking-new auction arena with holding pens, a monument to positive thinking. It was built by a nonprofit consortium of local ranchers who joined forces with the BLM to manage the growing number of wild horses decimating the rangeland on Beatys Butte, rangeland the ranchers depended on for grazing cattle. Some maintain the BLM's enforcement of cattle grazing regulations would never have allowed for such blatant and egregious excess as was taking place with wild horses. Others feel horses are better regulated than cattle. But the facts are that the Beatys Butte Herd Management Area (HMA), which was permitted for 250 horses, was carrying over 1,500. That the effort and expense of the auction was aimed at the hoped-for sale of only 10 horses might seem like spitting in the ocean, but the organizers saw the initial effort as more symbolic than anything, bringing regional attention to the crisis and illustrating a possible way out of it.

The wild-horse problem is duplicated on BLM lands across the West and is well represented in the documentary *Unbranded*, the story of four young men who purchase at auction and then break and train wild BLM horses to ride from Mexico to Canada, staying on public lands the whole way. The film persuasively underscores the urgent need for better management of these growing herds juxtaposed with the conflicting demands on the rangelands by cattle interests and environmental groups, interested in a more holistic approach than giving the horses free range (no pun intended) allows. In the film, one rancher in nearby Jefferson County has watched as grasslands, creeks, and springs are destroyed by the wild horses. Frustrated by his efforts to bring the BLM's attention to the problem, he complains: "You might as well send your letters to Santa Claus at the North Pole."

How did this get started? In 1971, when the Wild Free-Roaming Horses and Burros Act was passed, language in the act elevated the "invasive" and "nuisance" animals of the grazing service era to "the living symbols of the old West." The BLM was assigned to manage the new program as most of the alleged wild horses and burros were on BLM lands, and once again the beleaguered BLM was embroiled in a worsening and costly situation they did not want to be in.

When I was ranching, it was common knowledge that townsfolk who couldn't afford to keep a horse, or rodeo concessionaires who had bucking stock that wouldn't buck anymore, or anyone with old, unwanted horses would turn them out on the open range. But advocacy groups across the country have anthropomorphized these horses. This is fueled by the fact that during a routine BLM roundup of wild horses in southeastern Oregon in 1977, a BLM employee noticed primitive marks on some, "resembling horses as they existed back to the Ice Age and to a very high degree representing a type of horse brought to this country by the Spaniards." Subsequent tests showed this to be, in fact, true. Telltale markings include the dorsal stripe, or lineback, down the back of the Kiger and the zebra stripes on their legs. The Kiger is small, fourteen hands or so, with hard feet and incredible physical endurance. Their coloring ranges from dun, claybank (white), darker brown, grulla (gray/brown) to honey-colored, and interestingly they segregate according to color. The Kiger are known to scorn other wild horses and have managed to keep the integrity of their breed intact; although recently their numbers are being dangerously overwhelmed by other breeds turned out on the desert. The legendary stallion of the high desert's Kiger herd is *mesteño*, which means "unclaimed horse" in Spanish. Most Kigers' bloodlines are traced to this one horse who lived his whole life on Steens Mountain. Today the Kigers are a tourist attraction. City slickers, or "goat ropers" as they are pejoratively referred to by cowboys, drive out into the high desert with their cameras poised to record a fleeting glimpse of the offspring of mesteño.

But regardless of their origin, to wild-horse advocates every one of these horses—castaways or Kigers—is truly wild and answer some innate human need to believe wildness exists somewhere, even though our daily habits as humans kill it. They are seen as symbols of freedom, as descendants of the horses brought from Spain before the West was settled. According to a 2013 article for *CBS News* by Brian Montopoli, horses have been slaughtered for food in the United States as recently as 2006, but mostly for export to Asia and Europe. When food was rationed during World War II, horse meat was a solution. In 1951 *Time* magazine reported that horse meat was an important ingredient in Oregon cuisine. Now, despite the fact that millions of humans are starving across the planet, wild-horse advocates have lobbied for and succeeded in the passage of more and more laws eliminating options for disposing of wild horses. Managing herd numbers is nearly impossible.

A balanced approach to rangeland use can provide what everyone wants and needs. But if any one demand is given lopsided priority and a blind eye is turned toward resource management, all hell breaks loose. The fact is nearly fifty thousand horses are in holding pens across the West in an effort to relieve rangeland. This comes at a cost of $47 million to taxpayers to house, feed, and care for them. At the most, five thousand a year are placed nationally through wild-horse adoption programs and auctions. Steven Spielberg set a record in 1999 when he paid a reported $50,000 for a three-year-old stallion, after which he modeled the movie *Spirit, Stallion of the Cimarron*, released three years later. Now it's more typical for the BLM to offer an incentive of $1,000 if an individual agrees to take a horse. The on-range wild-horse and burro population is increasing by 7.5 percent a year. It doubled between 2012 and 2018 to eighty-two thousand.

The auction started Friday afternoon with a preview of the ten horses available for adoption, followed by a horse-training demonstration. The actual sale would take place the next day. Interested buyers had to qualify to adopt a wild mustang, and help with the paperwork was available. The buyer had to be at least eighteen years old, and the animal had to remain in the United States until the certificate of title was received from the BLM. The buyer could have no record of inhumane treatment of animals or violations of the 1971 Wild Free-Roaming Horses and Burros Act and must have adequate feed, water, and facilities (four hundred square feet per animal).

The auction flyer indicated that the two-year-old horses available for auction were "green broke" with an average of a hundred hours of training each. That means the young man I was in line with at the bank had been on these ten horses for a total of one thousand hours. It was emphasized that the horses would need further training although their "education" to date included being loaded into trailers, ridden in all weather and terrain, and exposed to cattle, dogs, and traffic. Interested buyers strolled past the holding pens, the names of each horse painted on a sign suspended from the crossbar: Oly, Barry, Lefty, Flash Gordon, Purple, El Chapo, Chuck Wagon, Tuko, Poncho, Chili. Walking past them, I looked into their large dark eyes. I projected on to their burr-ridden, tangled manes, their scruffy coats, the scars on their hides from altercations within the herd, the hardships of life they must have endured in the wilds, the cost of freedom. I imagined them curried and combed, coats glistening, on a bed of clean straw. I extended my palm for them to smell, nuzzle. I soon had my favorites.

✦

It's a given that children growing up on a ranch participate in 4-H. And it is suggested, though never heeded, that it's easier on the future farmer or rancher not to name their animal, the one your child sleeps with in the stall, feeds, brushes, hugs, loves—because the whole point is that the animals go to auction and are sold to slaughter, the meat cut and wrapped for the buyer, and the proceeds used to buy clothes for school or save for a first car or for college. Naming things renders them human. We ate Push and Shove, our two beloved pigs that I fed and cared for. We slaughtered, dressed, cut, and wrapped our own beef. The wife of a nearby rancher had a giant pet sow who would waddle freely into the room of her ranch house she had converted into a hair salon. As we baked in rollers under the space-age hair dryers, the sow would lean her Mini

Cooper–sized body against the chair, rubbing her bristly hind end up and down on the arm. We'd obligingly scratch her behind her pink ear. She wound up as bacon.

I loved my chickens, started my day calling "Here chick, chick!" as I scattered corn to my grateful hens Henny Penny, Biscuit, Queenie, Tallulah. I had an egg run, delivering eggs to distant neighbors. But when the time came, I slaughtered the hens that had quit laying. With a clothes hanger bent to a hook, I'd sneak up on the hen grubbing in the yard and snag her by a leg. Upside down, she'd surrender, wings flung overhead, her small brain topsied, hunt-and-peck turvied, the sky suddenly underfoot. I'd right-side her, smooth her feathers, tuck her under my arm, slowly stroke her beak between lizard-lidded eyes till she was spellbound. Then I'd flop her thin neck across the stump and, with the kitchen hatchet, chop off her decorated pate.

It's true what they say about running around like a chicken with its head cut off, lifeblood spilling over the bare ground, involuntarily carrying on, without thought, plan, or direction—but looking for all the world like a living thing playing itself out. I'd kick the dogs away, grab the witless squab, dunk her in the steaming pot to loosen the hold of her dimpled skin, and then spank her like a newborn. Thickets of soggy down would fall around my feet. Naked as the day is new, she was now ready to be gutted: tiny insides removed, tiny heart and remains of cricket and corn, gizzards and cluck box—when pressed offering one last word. Soon the hen I'd fed and tendered and loved is on the counter, pink and clean, little drumstick arms extended, weighing in the same as the neighbor's preemie. My children liked to play with the severed, rubbery legs, pull the tendons, and watch the trident toes curl; they'd learn a thing or two about contraction, putting food on the table, voluntary and involuntary reaction.

I told Dr. Stuart Garrett, a naturalist in Bend, that when he identified an endangered succulent, *Botrychium pumicola*, near what is now the Newberry Crater National Monument, it had a face only a botanist could love. But that sweet, vulnerable face gained an identity, was successfully anthropomorphized, and became the poster plant and impetus for what resulted in the preservation of fifty-four thousand acres of parkland when the Newberry National Volcanic Monument was designated in 1990, with Garrett leading the charge as chairman.

Our compassion for things not human is closely related to anthropomorphism. If we can project a human quality onto something, we are more inclined to help it or save it. The most dangerous leaders dehumanize fellow humans—migrants and people of color or different faiths. What about plants, birds, and animals? Thus far we have pretty much managed to avoid projecting human qualities onto pigs, sheep, and cows. God help the rangelands when we see cows as having personalities. God help your breakfast egg when you channel your inner chicken. God help us feed the world when everything with eyeballs takes on human qualities.

My street in Bend is near a busy east–west arterial that moves traffic across the growing city. Often deer, a plague within the city limits, will get hit and make their way to die in my backyard. It used to be there was no assistance available. I'd have to watch and wait for the animal to take its last breath, roll the body onto a tarp, and haul it to the curb for the sheriff's department to come and retrieve it. Now I can call the Bend police who are now authorized to shoot a critically injured deer that is at death's door, unable to move. I still have to get the animal to the curb, but at least its suffering is less protracted, sometimes. I called the police recently because of a buck in my yard that was seriously injured, listless, not moving as it lay on the ground, for three days. The officer walked brusquely around the corner of my house and toward the deer. He startled the suffering animal, who made a desperate effort to struggle to its feet. The officer apologized and said he couldn't help after all. As long as the deer was able to get up, he couldn't put it down. He had to respect the "natural process."

Let's think about this. People have planted things in town that attract deer, some even feed them; housing projects have interfered with deer habitat and migratory routes; streets and cars and neighborhoods aren't exactly part of the natural process. Let's think about this. Was the deer desperate, suffering?

Where does this leave us? Dog farms in Asia are seized by well-meaning groups from the United States. But the projection of our culture's economically secure, well-fed human emotions on those dogs removes a source of available meat for people in need of inexpensive sources of protein. And what happens to the dogs once they are in the United States? There is no shortest distance between two points when it comes to all of this, but it seems to me that putting our privileged compassion ahead of humans without enough food is wrong. Jane Fonda remarked in a presentation in Seattle that we seem to be more concerned about whether the chicken we are eating is organic than we are about making sure everyone has something to eat.

Ranching is increasingly restricted by environmental and animal rights legislation along with the changing land-use designations in the BLM West (Oregon, Nevada, Idaho, Wyoming, and Utah), where the total land mass administered by federal agencies is at least 50 percent of the total state acres. Are those who have no trouble putting food on their table, who have little boots-on-the-ground understanding of what it takes to do so, having a disproportionate influence on land-use policies and animal rights?

Starving range, animals, people. The day after the horse sale, a cow skull mounted on the crossbar high above the entrance to the auction arena was stark against the blue, cloudless sky. Wind whistled plaintively through the empty metal barn, scattering discarded auction flyers and the associated unanswered questions across the hard ground.

ELEVEN

Re-create

I WAS INVITED TO brave the cold and huddle with friends around a burn pit filled with a summer's worth of grass clippings and fall's pruned branches. A skiff of snow decorated brittle brown stalks of wild rye and the willows' bare purple branches. To help get the bonfire going, I contributed a copy of the *Source*, Bend's groovy news-weekly listing a gazillion things to do in town, an event-a-minute, concert-a-minute, restaurant and movie reviews, quirky astrological forecasts, hikes and camping destinations, new mountain bike routes.

The outings recommended in the *Source* bleed farther and farther into the high desert as consumers of wilderness love the Cascades to death. There is increased pressure on open spaces in central and southeastern Oregon and increased pressure on the BLM to reimagine the uses for the wilderness it manages as rural economies falter. Some in the hinterlands view these new consumers—from dirt bikers to McRanchers to corporate acquisitions of high-desert acreage to green energy developers—as marauders, worthy of suspicion; others see them as a boon, a potential source of revenue for remote communities.

Of course, wilderness has been commercialized and harvested for centuries, starting with coveted arrowheads and pelts, rangeland used by sheep and cattle, timber and mining interests that extracted everything from gravel to geothermal, from bentonite to Glass Butte obsidian, sunstones to saline. Now, on BLM lands, a new harvest of natural resources is in the spotlight as logging and grazing exit stage right, undermined by environmental organizations. With a stated goal of twenty thousand megawatts of renewable energy produced on public lands by 2020, the BLM opened Renewable Energy Coordination offices across the West in 2009 to approve and oversee wind, solar, biomass, and geothermal projects. A year later the first utility-scale solar energy projects were approved, and by 2014, solar energy projects covering nearly six hundred thousand acres had been proposed, those underway generating light for nearly three million homes. Negative impacts? Yes. Large expanses of ground become inaccessible to wildlife and inhospitable to plant life. Though this doesn't happen with residential photovoltaic solar power panels, birds' wings have been seared off when they flew too close to vast fields of solar mirrors used in large utility-scale installations. Contrary to what Kermit the Frog maintained, it appears it is easier to get government permission if you're green. How green are they? Maybe it's safer to say "greener" energy.

It's my impression that the tougher scrutiny is reserved for ranchers using BLM land for grazing with the result that grazing is probably one of the better managed uses of BLM ground. The justified questioning of solar or wind hasn't claimed much airtime despite the requirement that all BLM decisions have to be made in the public interest, and change requests affecting federal land management must be reviewed by the National Environmental Policy Act, passed in 1970. There's growing concern that savvy environmental and entrepreneurial land-use groups circumvent the BLM and other government land agencies in order to fast-track policy at the congressional level, thereby avoiding BLM requirements for site assessments and public input. And this trend will be exacerbated by moving BLM headquarters to Colorado, as announced in 2019 by William Pendley, deputy director for BLM policy and programs under President Donald Trump.

Solar isn't the only new kid on the BLM block. There are sixty and counting geothermal leases in producing status on BLM lands representing 40 percent of the geothermal energy capacity in the United States. How about the woody biomass coming off public timberlands? The use of these materials as a renewable resource is developing, albeit slowly. In Lakeview, Red Rock Biofuels will soon process wood material when it comes online, and it's anticipated the plant will spawn related industries. With the 2018 congressional approval of hemp production and the anticipated federal legalization of marijuana, stay tuned for the latest on the incursion of these new economic options on public land.

The BLM also manages over twenty million acres of public lands that have "wind potential" that could power more than two million homes. The worst environmental impact of the turbines is not the noise pollution or the bird and bat deaths; rather, it is the unsightly intrusion of these behemoths whirling atop every pristine ridge and, heretofore, unfettered flat. They are otherworldly monuments to our unbridled consumption, sense of entitlement, and lack of discipline. Thankfully, most of the ODT territory and the spectacularly wild country it includes has so far been spared, the outback of Oregon thankfully lacking the necessary transmission infrastructure.

As the sun and wind are harnessed for our needs, it's worth remembering that pretty much everything man has conscripted into his service has resulted in collateral damage and, in some cases, has been depleted if not exhausted. Environmentalist Bill McKibben opines, in his book *Deep Economy*, that ethics and economy go hand in hand. The old "follow the money." There are choices regarding rural America's—all of America's—economic future, but our appetites must change for the choices to be most effective. What is it about moderation in all things that we don't understand? Can we switch from more, more, more to enough already? Metaphorically I can't help but wonder what the world would be like without wind after we have used it all up. Let's hope this *is* a metaphor. But we never thought it possible to deplete our oceans or to pollute the night sky.

All this notwithstanding, the fact is, rural Oregon needs income, needs jobs. Small town main streets have as many empty storefronts as occupied ones. Ginger Casto came back to her native Lakeview after earning a degree in the social sciences and psychology, a stint in the Peace Corps, a career running nonprofits in larger communities, and raising a family. She was appointed the economic development coordinator for the Southern Oregon Economic Development District. She returned to a town a bit tattered at the edges, but she was home. With a giveback mentality she inherited from her parents (and typical of residents of small communities), she does everything. "My job is to coordinate projects that benefit the county in the area of economic development. I work diligently with the Chamber of Commerce on tourism, helped found the Main Street Program . . . instrumental in bringing back the Alger Theater . . . to help make our downtown more appealing and give the community a cultural outlet for movies, performances, and so on. I am active in Rotary—I am the incoming president—and on the County Planning Commission. I volunteer for various other community events and groups. I feel a part of something comfortable and worthwhile."

The new economies have the formidable assignment of reversing rural America's sharp decline as the population in these communities gets poorer, more frustrated, and according to Alissa Quartz, the author of *Squeezed: Why Our Families Can't Afford America*, ashamed of their circumstances, their debt, and their inability to find work despite a college degree or vocational training. The lumber mill and forest jobs are gone. Government jobs are hard to find. Ranches and farms are providing fewer employment opportunities. Too often drugs are the answer. Lakeview, like many communities across the nation, is grappling with the opioid epidemic. The unemployed and underemployed are angry and want to blame someone. They feel powerless, invisible. They want a cause. But these feelings lead them to taking action in wrong and self-destructive ways or lining up behind false prophets.

On the high desert today ranching generates the greatest annual profit followed by timber. Of those revenues the BLM returns 50 percent to the host counties, chiefly to be used for public school funding and road repair. The newer harvest industries will hopefully follow this giveback equation and, in combination, all will play nice on public lands. Take what is needed and leave the rest. If not, as attributed to Alanis Obomsawin of the Odanak Reserve in Canada, "When the last tree has been cut down, the last fish caught, the last river poisoned, only then will we realize that one cannot eat money."

In rides the knight in shining armor astride his white horse, his chain mail made of Lycra; his shield, a knapsack-cum-water bottle; his sword, a set of telescoping hiking poles; his horse, a fat-tire mountain bike. His parlance? It could go something like this: "I can't bonk, not now. I'm not willing to register anything close to a nero.

Plus, I have to make the next restock. I'm out of mountain money and a cat hole is calling me. Call me a gearhead, but my wet feet would kill for a pair of quick-wicking socks. It would sure help matters if GBITS would ease up on the snow and sleet." To translate, *bonk* is when you run out of energy in a long race or on a long hike due to not eating enough calories; *nero* is a word you don't hear often among thru-hikers as it designates an almost-zero or a short mileage day; *GBITS* is the Great Backpacker in the Sky who throws impossible challenges in the way of backpackers to test their fortitude; *gear head*—we all know at least one whose primary focus is having all the latest equipment and clothing; *mountain money* is toilet paper and a *cat hole* is dug in the ground to deposit human waste.

I don't mean to make fun. Remember, I am a self-proclaimed geezer jock. We all wear the uniform of our beliefs, our circumstances. We all have a persona that we nurture and cherish, from the high-performance athlete to the birder, from the cowboy who just found the hat to the seasoned rancher. The real issue, as Brent Fenty reminds, is that there aren't enough places set aside for all the different types of users.

At an ONDA environmental conference in 2012, I attended a panel discussion titled "Wilderness, Good for Business." The presenters talked about wilderness as a commodity, to be sold and consumed according to rules that preserve it and keep it wild. Wilderness economics. "Protected wild places are important to the outdoor industry," says John Sterling, past president of the Conservation Alliance. "This is the infrastructure of outdoor recreation. Their customers need these places to use the products they make and sell." Videographer Jason Bagby, founder of the Cascadia Adventure Film Festival, teamed up with Visit Bend in 2019 to produce a film that focuses on high-desert "areas of dispersement that need traffic." Is it possible to consume and preserve at once? And tourism—it doesn't extract anything? Doesn't degrade a natural resource?

Christopher Ketcham refers to recreation as the newest frontier of "wilderness compromise" in a 2014 *Orion* magazine article, "Taming the Wilderness." He cites the Oregon Badlands Wilderness as a case study of wilderness marketed as a recreational commodity, pointing to the fact that the Bend-based Conservation Alliance—representing the interests of outdoor gear and manufacturing industries such as REI, Patagonia, Columbia, Kelty, Keen, and Clif Bar—lobbied for the creation of the wilderness. Ketcham grieves that wilderness as the infrastructure for profit-making turns it into nothing more than an economic engine. Protecting what is truly wild is "a realm of human experience outside the confines of the commercial mindset," which Ketcham files under "growthmania."

Ranchers bordering the Oregon Desert Trail are saying the same thing in a different way. One rancher sees the trail as a "gateway drug" for more and more public incursion, more and more restrictions on the ranching way of life. Another compares the trail to the railroad coming into the West, a means of civilizing southeastern Oregon, of introducing a different population with different priorities. In a 2018 *Oregon Business* article, "Walking on a Knife's Edge," author Caleb Diehl states that ranchers in Lake County "don't have a problem with the trail as is, but they fear designation could pave the way for scenic buffers up to a quarter mile on each side. In those buffer zones, agencies could ban motorized use and grazing. Along the Pacific Crest Trail, land trusts have succeeded in converting private land to public to make buffers that preserve a natural experience and allow easier access."

Whether it's politics, policy, or politesse, Oregon Natural Desert Association's ODT manager Renee Patrick acknowledges that portions of the trail in the Fremont-Winema National Forest, the Pueblo Mountains, and Steens Mountain have received land-use designations, but she maintains ONDA is no longer actively pursuing designation for the rest of the route with the caveat that "nothing is off the table, but we're trying to think this through thoughtfully. Our goal is to have a route that stays in harmony with the landscape, livelihoods, and habitats as much as possible." In "Walking on a Knife's Edge," Diehl spoke to Adel rancher John O'Keefe, who says, "They make it up as some big deal. If somebody wants to go out there and walk, they can walk there now. Don't have to make a big effort to make it a trail." This sentiment was echoed by a rancher that thru-hiker Ryan "Dirtmonger" Sylva reported as saying, "They want to make this area a monument, and I ain't seen anyone out here but you."

Lakeview reports a slight increase in visitation numbers thanks to the ODT, with most hiking shorter sections rather than tackling the thru-hike. But Ginger Casto sees tourism trends starting to get a foothold "whether the county and their communities are ready for them or not. Travel Oregon has been working to begin marketing and pushing out all those wonderful well-hidden secrets of our county into the western portion of the state. We are definitely noticing a difference." This includes the recent addition of the Timber Trail, which opened in 2017 for mountain bikers. It, too, is bringing some tourism traffic to the county. A 670-mile backcountry route from the Columbia River to the California border, the Timber Trail travels through US Forest Service lands, including a section of the Fremont National Forest that traverses Winter Ridge before heading through Paisley and into the Warner Mountains near Lakeview.

There's something "no there there" about the phrase "tourism economy." It strikes me as an oxymoron or a fancy Ponzi scheme, panning for fool's gold. We are essentially harvesting ourselves. No limit in sight on the production of selves. No problem so long as there is sufficient disposable income and fossil fuel to get us where we want to go. I seem to be among the few who question tourism as the panacea. Worldwide, it is seen as the path to economic salvation. For rural high-desert communities, the Oregon Tourism Commission's Travel Oregon campaign has coined the Rural Tourism Studio, a program that provides rural communities with "guidance, training, and support" for regional attractions. Their pitch includes the invitation to create big-picture strategies and to dive deep to create new tourism offerings, from outdoor recreation (code for hunting and riding ATVs and dirt bikes) to bicycle tourism, hawking cultural to agricultural heritage. Community members participate in six to eight full-day workshops over the course of four months. The result? Action teams. Meetings. A shot at various grants. Small communities are getting on board and hopes are high, but three years in, rural wallets are not much fatter.

The audiences targeted for rural tourism offerings fall along the lines of the urban-rural divide, politics, and even skin color. Green tourists (hikers, cyclists, birders) turn up their noses at the motorized or armed sector and vice versa. The tourism brochures, however, don't discriminate, grouping together ads for riding ATVs through the BLM's eleven thousand acres of sixty-foot-high sand dunes near Christmas Valley, hunting in the forests atop Winter Ridge, and fishing in the Ana or Chewaucan Rivers alongside the more benign offerings: bird-watching in Summer Lake Wildlife Refuge or Malheur National Wildlife Refuge, floating the Owyhee River with the Oregon Natural Desert Association, or hiking in Fort

Rock, Crack-in-the-Ground, Steens Mountain, and the Pueblos. Fifth wheels, motor homes, and camper vans are common on rural two-lane highways. And increasingly four-wheel drive camper vans are heading off-road. I find it ironic that most trailers and campers are emblazoned with the names of what we're endangering: gray wolf, meerkat, bighorn, wildcat, cougar, arctic fox, raptor, and so on.

The democratic brochures are a vote for all these pursuits to exist side by side. And they likely can if we're clever and open-minded and don't lose our sense of humor. For a number of years, I participated in Logan's Run in Oregon's Strawberry Mountains, a cross-country ski race hosted by Prairie City's local snowmobile group. It's legend that snowmobilers and cross-country skiers are like oil and water. One is viewed as requiring noisy machines that burn fossil fuel, and the other seen as a recipe for no fun favoring self-flagellation in the form of skiing uphill on skinny skis for miles and miles. But for this race, judgments were set aside once a year. The snowmobile club set and groomed the ski tracks. At the hydration stops, the club's volunteers served hot coffee and frosting-covered doughnuts, a departure from the usual Gatorade and PowerBar, as if to say, "Get over yourselves, you hyper loonies! We're here to set you straight." The gourmet post-race banquet the snowmobilers put on for racers was beyond compare. And for dessert? Community, comradery, and a good laugh about high fructose bear claws replacing PowerGels.

The climb is steep for recreational tourism or any form of tourism to economically overtake farming and ranching, which are still the primary economic drivers in eastern Oregon. Livestock alone generated $900 million in 2018. The ODT is expected to attract twenty thru-hikers a year. Do the math.

If the outdoors is going to succeed as an economic solution for rural communities, work has to be done to attract the large, untapped urban population that eschews freezing for fun, getting blisters for fun, feeling unwelcome for fun. The out-of-doors is predominantly a white person's playground. Between 2008 and 2012, 95 percent of those backpacking in national forests and wilderness areas were white. There are economic barriers, yes, but mainly it's a cultural mind-set on both sides of the equation. Rural communities in the West aren't known for rolling out the red carpet for people of color.

Ginger Casto places her hopes for more tolerance in the college-educated youth returning to the county, but they need jobs. "There are literally no jobs except service-oriented jobs for them, although some have the option of joining agriculture/livestock businesses or larger industry businesses that are owned by their families." She is also counting on the return of people like herself. "What is more interesting to me is people like me who have been away for ten, twenty, or forty years and are returning. I have many classmates that are retiring and moving back. Or even younger in their mid-fifties. They are opening home-based businesses or just enjoying coming back and being involved in the community. Many have been, like me, always yearning to get back. Things change in their lives, and they come home."

Not far behind recreational tourism is cultural tourism. Casto's efforts to revitalize the Alger Theater in Lakeview is an example and so is PLAYA as it launches programs to partner with regional organizations to spread the cultural wealth thanks to the artists and scientists who retreat to the sixty-five-acre campus. Summer Lake Hot Springs hosts an annual concert in conjunction with Paisley's Mosquito Festival that includes parade floats displaying ginormous mosquitos fashioned of rebar (antennae) and heating ducts (body). Parade participants circle town twice so the parade isn't over too fast. Maybe Paisley will become the Oregon version of Marfa, Texas, reinventing its middle-of-nowhere self into an arts and cultural hub.

My contribution to tourist excursions into the desert is long-weekend writing workshops. I traditionally schedule a retreat in mid-August, the same time as the Perseid meteor shower, awe-inspiring when viewed where the night sky is perfectly black. I lease facilities on a large, isolated ranch able to accommodate ten to twelve in a house-turned-lodge. The week after the meteor shower happens to be the opening of hunting season. On the last day of the workshop, my bespectacled, Birkenstocked writers pack up binoculars, bird and plant identification books, journals, laptops, files marked "haiku" or "writing exercises," and head home, gingerly navigating their Prius over rocks and potholes and the miles of dirt road to the highway. They are likely to pass, going the other way, jacked-up pickups on enormous tires with six-packs of beer on the back seat, gun racks across the back window, spotting scopes, coolers, tents, and gear stashed under a tarp in the bed of the truck, and drivers dressed in camo and wearing aviator sunglasses. Swerving to avoid a collision, one eyes the other with equal parts surprise, suspicion, and the good news, curiosity.

One year the cook at the lodge was the son of the concessionaire. Generally, the facility is only available to fishing and hunting groups, but during the off-season I am lucky to be able to use it for my work-shop. I invite participants to bring a favorite book with them to share on the first evening as a way of breaking the ice and getting to know one another. The sitting area is separated from the kitchen by a counter. On this occasion the cook, toiling over the stove, was plainly not pleased to have been assigned to this geeky group of writers and poets. He far preferred the company of hunters. Or so he thought.

One writer from California had forgotten to bring a reading selection. A very attractive older woman, dressed the ranch part in never-before-worn jeans, western shirt, and bandanna around her neck, offered a book she authored and self-published: *A Vintage Year.* He could read from it if he wanted. He politely obliged her, randomly opened it, and started to read. It was the sexiest, most graphic love scene any of us had ever heard, including the cook in the kitchen who pulled off his cap and started fanning himself as the recitation continued. When it was over, we all hooted and cheered the author who sat demurely with a cat-that-ate-the-canary look. The cook took the opportunity to lean out over the counter and announce: "If that were my book, I'd take it with me to bed ever' night and, by damn, them pages would be stuck together!" We told the author that was the best review she'd ever get. It should go on the back cover as a blurb. After this initiation, the camp cook was happy to be on hand for subsequent writing retreats. Open-mindedness is not a form of weakness.

By now, the bonfire is nothing more than smoldering coals. Large, lazy flakes of snow hiss as they land. We stare out across the embers to a gun-metal evening sky crepe-papered with the sunset's orange and red. Behind us, an unobstructed view of Slide Mountain's precipitously steep escarpment. In front, a frozen-solid Summer Lake, a perfect icy confection where the day before I had skated to eternity. Saying nothing we spontaneously raise our thermoses, toasting the miracle that such a place could exist, and selfishly, that for now so few of us are here to enjoy it.

TWELVE

Feathers and Fins

A s we've been sitting around debating the pros and cons of various options for rural revitalization, ODT hikers have long since started up Abert Rim. If you thought Winter Ridge was an impressive scarp, this one is spectacular. It is thirty miles long and one of the highest in the United States, rising a dramatic twenty-five hundred feet off the valley floor to a fifty-six-hundred-foot summit that overlooks the saline Lake Abert. It's tiring to get to the top, but the views are to die for, which you'll feel you just very nearly did. From there it's more wide-open sage country as the ODT heads to Plush. It can claim a general store but not much else. Adel, thirty-one miles off course, is more desirable for restocking with a motel, café, and market. There isn't another opportunity to resupply, refuel, or revive until Frenchglen, another seventy-two miles of challenging high-desert terrain. On your way you'll traverse a section of the Hart Mountain National Antelope Refuge, a 278,000-acre cattle-free sanctuary of wildflowers, pronghorn, and bighorn sheep. Climb thirty-six hundred feet to the top of Hart Mountain for a view of the Warner Valley and wetlands where, it's said, Cheryl Strayed holed up to finish *Wild*. Once again, this dramatic escarpment produces a delicious hot spring, a ten-by-fifteen-foot pool of bubbling 105-degree water, where most hikers congregate. Some would say the many hot springs along the ODT are better than an Airbnb. That includes me.

Botanist and environmentalist Dr. Stuart Garrett is quick to say that Hart Mountain didn't always spoil our eyes with broad vistas of native shrubs and grasses, the whole area now a healthy, thriving water-retaining sponge. In the '80s, he points out, the Guano drainage that feeds Hart Mountain was essentially dried up. The refuge, created in 1936, was initially for the protection of remnant herds of pronghorn with grazing of domestic cattle continuing unchecked. In response to evidence of overstocking, in the 1970s a best-laid plan was adopted that featured controlled grazing as a method to restore the refuge and to encourage natural plant growth. But it didn't work. The stream bank erosion, the associated loss of streamside vegetation to guard healthy water temperatures, and continued degradation of plants due to the presence of cattle led, in 1989, to the creation of a new management plan approved five years later that included—not without a lot of wrangling between ranchers and environmentalists—the removal of feral horses and domestic cattle and a commitment to the protection of native habitat to support native wildlife. Diametrically opposed to cattle on public land, Garrett played a big role in advocating for the creation of this cattle-free refuge. The before and after images are staggering, he remarks. And now? "No question. Hart feels like home." Justice William O. Douglas expressed a similar sentiment: "I always feel sad leaving Hart Mountain. Yet after I travel a few hours and turn to see its great bulk against a southern sky my heart rejoices. This refuge will leave our grandsons and granddaughters an inheritance of the wilderness that no dollars could recreate. Here they will find life teeming throughout all the life zones that lead from the desert to alpine meadows."

Typical of what, by now, is a given along the rough and the smooth of the ODT, the next stretch to Frenchglen is a long passage through challenging sagebrush desert terrain, more than earning hikers a night in the Frenchglen Hotel, an old pension-style hotel at the foot of Steens Mountain, the gateway to the Malheur National Wildlife Refuge. I fell in love early on with this maze of emerald greenery in the spring; the knee-buckling canvas of russet, amber, ochre in the fall; of meadows, dikes, marshes, the cacophony of thousands of birds—to me a high-desert Eden.

I was first there as a chaperone to the students from my children's rural two-room elementary school on field trips. We stayed overnight in the Quonset huts at the Malheur Field Station, and during the day at the refuge we made imprints of bird tracks with moist wads of clay, checked off refuge plants and birds in coloring books their teacher had made, visited the manicured grounds of the refuge headquarters, and explored the elegant, old buildings built of red lava tuff with tall, quivering cottonwoods standing guard. Our young charges tried to but didn't succeed in evading the gaze of the glass-eyed birds mounted on the walls or that of the enormous taxidermied trumpeter swan flying overhead, suspended by a string. They pressed their noses against the glass cases of arrowheads and bark mats on display. It felt like discovery for us all, that heady sensation that creates ownership, caring, the desire to protect.

I was lucky to be part of two writing workshops at Malheur Field Station under the tutelage of Ursula Le Guin, the refuge as textbook and inspiration. The first workshop with her, in that place, had been a breakthrough for many of us as writers and life-changing in ways we would only appreciate over time, if ever. Two would end unhappy marriages. Three left their business careers to dedicate themselves to writing. Everything about our time there seemed like an altered reality—from all of us leaping into the unplumbed calderas of small volcanoes, our bodies piercing the slime-coated surface and disappearing into the magma-heated water, to lying spread-eagle on the ground at night, apprehending the silence, the star-filled sky, the chorus of coyotes. On the first day of the workshop at the field station campus, a magpie flew into the classroom, landed on my desk, and stayed. It did the same each day thereafter, gifting me with bits of glistening mica, remnants of a tire. I have these things still. It even hunted for me down the long line of bunkbeds in the Quonset hut dormitory. I watched it hopping confidently down the middle of the large room, cocking its head this way and that until it spotted me. I confess I grew a bit spooked by the bird's attention. I am sure there are explanations. Perhaps the magpie had been spoiled by visitors, was seeking food, a handout. But under the thrall of this desert place, I felt the magpie was a visitor from another world trying to make contact. What was it trying to tell me?

The second workshop was some years later, with Le Guin as well as poet and memoirist Judith Barrington. No visitations from the magpie this time but, as unforgettable, a forest fire burning far to the east, unusual for its size. It lit up the night.

Those memories of visits to Eden, honing my beginner birding skills, searching for the elusive Kiger mustangs, looking down on the Alvord Desert from the ten-thousand-foot edge of Steens Mountain, I now realize, were before Adam, Eve, the apple, or the snake showed up. First dates. I clung to my perception of this being a peaceable kingdom, but, as life teaches, as we get to know a place, a person, the first-blush projections are hard to sustain.

It was primarily the Wadatika band for whom this marshland was the center of the universe, whose nomadic seasonal rounds in search of root and berry, wild game and fish rippled concentrically out from this lush place. The arrival of white settlers in the mid-1800s marked the beginning of the Northern Paiute's protracted suffering, their numbers decimated by war, Eurasian diseases, and starvation as they were shuttled from pillar to post, treaties made and broken again and again. Sarah Winnemucca, a Northern Paiute, described the early years of European contact in her memoir *Life Among the Paiutes: Their Wrongs and Claims* and traveled the United States to advocate for Native American rights. But in the end, the 1.5 million acres of the Northern Paiutes' original Oregon tribal lands were reduced by treaty to a paltry 760 acres that finally, in 1972, was designated as the Burns Paiute Reservation by the federal government. The settlement amount for lands taken away, negotiated over nine decades, amounted to a whopping $743.20 to each tribal member. Don't forget that twenty cents.

After the Bannock War of 1878 and the last of the Northern Paiutes were removed, ranchers grabbed the confiscated lands for cattle grazing and farming. Aggressive irrigation and marshland drainage projects went unchecked and tampered with precious water resources. Ironically it wasn't these bold encroachments that eventually got the attention of the federal government and resulted in the protection of the refuge. No. It was ladies' fashion. In the late nineteenth and early twentieth century, women in Chicago, New York City, and San Francisco didn't just favor feathered hats—they did not leave the house without one on their heads. Woe to the egrets, the herons, and the gulls of Malheur country. Two intrepid Oregon photographers, William Finley and Herman Bohlman, had recorded the extraordinary number and variety of birds at Malheur before the rude irrigation projects, before the plume hunters. They later returned at the height of the feather frenzy and photographed evidence of the catastrophic decimation of entire bird populations. The successful plea for protection they made to President Theodore Roosevelt resulted in the creation, in 1908, of the Malheur National Wildlife Refuge, starting with 80,000 acres and growing over time to its present size of 187,000 acres. The evidence exposed on unwieldy five-by-seven glass plate negatives saved many wings. That's the feathers part.

You'd think the next challenge to this Eden, the next cause for armed conflict, would be cattle related. Nope. It was a fish. Carp, to be exact. As part of an effort to keep irrigation canals clean so the water could move through unobstructed, carp were introduced to the refuge's maze of canals and waterways in the 1920s to munch on canal-clogging freshwater plants. They took their job seriously. Thirty years later the first concerns were voiced that the gluttonous fish could be an ecological threat. Flash-forward to the present: "I mean, there are no birds," United States Fish and Wildlife biologist Linda Beck laments. This observation stands in stark contrast to that of Alice Elshoff, who, not many years earlier, noted that, floods and droughts at the Malheur notwithstanding, the birds kept coming. "They keep migrating from South America to the Arctic to Siberia, stitching the continents together."

They are still migrating but are now forced to find other stopping places for sustenance. The Malheur National Wildlife Refuge had long been a stopping-off point along the Pacific Flyway, where hundreds of varieties of birds breed and nest. Once among the most productive waterfowl breeding areas in the country and a rest stop for thousands of migrating birds, it is now a ghost-way. Waterfowl production is said to be down by 75 percent, and the visiting flocks, so large they used to darken the sky, forming feathered Milky Ways of sorts, have fallen by the millions. The carp, following their original marching orders, are devouring sago pondweed, and widgeon grass (staples of waterfowl diets), as well as insects and other food. The carp have colonized all of Lake Malheur. In addition to eating every water plant, they stir up silt when rooting on the lake's bottom, rendering the water too murky for sunlight to nurture the growth of the few lake grasses struggling to survive. No amount of rotenone poisonings or expensive removal efforts have made a dent. The population of these water pigs is said to be over a million, each mature female laying five hundred thousand eggs a year over the course of her thirty-year-long life. Sit by the lake and it is mere moments before you'll see the sinister dorsal fins of the carp slicing through the water.

In the spring of 2019, I visited the refuge headquarters following that year's Migratory Bird Festival. Malheur Lake was shockingly far from its usual shoreline. I doubted the claim of the volunteer in the gift shop who said the remaining snowmelt off Steens Mountain would fill it. Admittedly, year to year, the lake expands and contracts in size. It grows to seventy square miles or more with a large snowpack and can shrink to twenty acres (which is less than a square mile) during severe drought. But having just passed miles of flooded fields and greenery around Frenchglen, the dry lakebed felt wrong somehow, a feeling underscored by the throngs of birds mobbing the inadequate small pond in front of the refuge headquarters. Maybe the dearth of water will prove to be nature's effort to starve out the carp.

Speaking of the tourism economy, here's one. After a night in my tent I had breakfast at the Diamond Hotel, an alternative soft bed and good meal for end-to-enders, another term for thru-hikers. I engaged in conversation with a woman from Portland at a nearby table, there on what she described as a mother-and-son bonding trip: clubbing the hundreds of netted carp to death before they are thrown into a mass grave. Just the image for the family holiday greeting card. Solutions for the carcasses range from organic carp fertilizer to green energy biogas, but these carp-clubbing efforts seem on par with selling ten horses at a time to address a fifty thousand wild-horse problem. Another plague of our own distracted creation. By the way, those exotic colored koi in your backyard landscaped-to-perfection pond? Common carp. Don't let them anywhere near a natural waterway. That's the fin part.

Why weren't cattle public enemy number one? There were plenty of environmentalists and conservationists who would have liked to give them that honor, that is until the successful creation of a new management plan for the Malheur Refuge began in 2008. It has proved to be an exemplary model of reaching consensus with environmentalists, ONDA, ranchers, refuge management, government representatives from the BLM, US Fish and Wildlife, and the Paiute tribe all at the table. Taking five years to complete, and with an intended shelf life of fifteen years, it just goes to show that different interest groups and factions can arrive at a workable compromise.

David Bilyeu, a citizens' representative on the Steens Advisory Council for three three-year terms that ended in 2016, explains that Secretary of the Interior Bruce Babbitt under President Clinton was going to put Steens Mountain in a national park. But advocates for giving locals control through a proposed collaborative mechanism miraculously won out and was the genesis of the creation of the Steens Advisory Council as specified within the Steens Act itself. The advisory council couldn't have been more diverse in political and environmental makeup. The process, according to Bilyeu, was "amazing despite the contention in the room. People really wanted to hammer it out. Weren't necessarily polite. But had the will to do it, to create new and unique solutions that ultimately were written into the Steens Act." According to Bilyeu it bore fruit in the end. "There are bright points. It's a matter of finding them and letting people know there are those bright points of possibility out there." Maybe the peaceable kingdom I so wanted to believe in would prove true after all.

But what I couldn't get out of my head, when at the Malheur Field Station with Ursula Le Guin for the second time was the ominous, Armageddon-like orange glow on the eastern horizon each night. The sunsets to the west fanned their peacock reds and purples across the sky, then, on cue, disappeared below the horizon, dutifully punctuating the end of another day; but to the east—a trickster sun, a raging imposter that refused to set, refused to leave, crowding the next day's dawn, turning the world on its side.

THIRTEEN

What's Your Occupation?

THE MALHEUR NATIONAL WILDLIFE REFUGE is just that for hikers: a lush, green hammock strung between Hart and Steens Mountains, a respite before tackling the ten-thousand-foot Steens Mountain. The ascent—in fact nothing on the ODT—does not always go as planned as thru-hiker Heather "Anish" Anderson writes in her blog:

> One of the difficulties of completing the Oregon Desert Trail is
> hitting the right weather window for each of the unique areas. The
> Steens represents one of the biggest challenges since it doesn't melt
> out until July and [2017] was an especially high snow year. I opted
> to take the closed road to the summit rather than the dangerously
> flooded Big Indian Canyon. About six miles up I was surprised to
> encounter a juniper removal/restoration crew. They informed me
> there was approximately ten to twelve miles of snow to cross to
> reach the summit. Without an ice ax and with very tender feet, I

decided to accept a ride back to Frenchglen. [From there] this meant walking forty-five miles of paved highway to get to Fields. It was hard on the feet, but easier than sliding around in wet shoes.

After Steens Mountain, the challenges that make up the last half of the Oregon Desert Trail are, in some ways, the most difficult but also the most beautiful part of the trek: descending off Steens to the Alvord Desert, then to Fields, over the Pueblo Mountains kissing the border of Nevada, and finally into the Owyhee Canyonlands. But for right now, life is good. Life is now. A full belly and a good night's sleep on a real bed. Seated on the porch of the Frenchglen Hotel, feet resting on the railing, having sent off Facebook and Instagram posts, a hiker gazes out at an uninterrupted view of land and sky, of emerald green rice-patty-like fields, leisurely makes entries in a dog-eared journal and plots the next few days: an eighteen-miler to a campground on the southern flank of Steens Mountain, a challenging twenty-four-mile push to the summit, and afterward down, down Wildhorse Canyon to the Alvord Desert. A pilot preparing for takeoff: food supply, check; water, check; gear, check.

It's hard to believe from the vantage point of this porch and quietude that down the road is where the 2016 armed occupation of the Malheur National Wildlife Refuge took place; the site of an insurrection that at the end of the day reshaped the national conversation and the 2016 and 2020 presidential elections.

Anyone anywhere near a news source on January 2 of that year was suddenly transported to a sage- and snow-covered flat where a ragtag group led by Ammon Bundy had taken over the Malheur National Wildlife Refuge. The small outpost includes a gift shop, museum, information center, a few outbuildings, and well-maintained grounds. The quiet beauty of the place renders it a sanctuary and for many, including the Paiutes, sacred. Paiute tribal burial sites are located on the refuge grounds, and the tribe has entrusted the storage of sacred items to the refuge. In a *New York Times* article, former Burns Paiute chairwoman Charlotte Rodrigue said it best, because she knows it best: "I am not sympathetic with a group of armed individuals who want territory we have lived on for thousands of years to be 'returned' to the 'people of Oregon.'" That the Bundy group chose this location to occupy, which was shuttered for winter and in fact has little to do with the subject of their protest (BLM grazing issues), felt like a chickenshit move. The occupiers were mostly men, some wearing cowboy hats, giving new meaning to "I'm not a cowboy, I just found the hat," and all were armed, some more dangerous than others if criminal records are any indication. All the major newspapers and television networks descended on nearby Burns, Oregon. "The very idea—that two ill-informed men from Utah could travel to Harney County, Oregon, and cast themselves as the representatives of local interests—satisfies all the technical criteria for classification as very batty behavior," wrote Patty Limerick, chair of the Center of the American West at the University of Colorado, in the *Denver Post* in 2017.

The reason for the occupation was initially confusing even to the occupiers, but thanks to help from the media in tidying up the story, it soon resolved into a demand for the government to turn public lands back to the states. Equally as batty was that the media chose and was able to elevate the group's conflated protests—of a twenty-year-old dispute between BLM and Nevada rancher Cliven Bundy, Ammon's father, who owed the BLM $1 million in unpaid grazing fees and a Burns, Oregon, arson charge against a father and son after fires they set spread to public lands—into a story of international stature. No small feat. It raises the question of the media's role in hyping a spasm to a full-fledged, highly sensationalized earthquake that resulted in the tragic and avoidable death, assuming less hyped-up circumstances, of one of the protesters, not to mention providing Ammon Bundy with a script.

According to Hal Herring in a March 2016 *High Country News* article, these symbols of the American West, these Marlboro men, were hollowed-out misfits in search of a cause. They included a wacky techie, a former hippie, a couple recently moved from Wisconsin to Idaho, a welder, and a roofer from Georgia. The martyr of the take-over, LaVoy Finicum, paid the bills by taking care of foster children. Ammon Bundy was a car fleet manager. These were not working ranchers, not cowboys. As Herring and others at the occupation reported, all involved in the standoff played fast and loose with the interpretation of the US Constitution. Few had heard of the Taylor Grazing Act or had read any of a number of books—*Sacred Cows at the Public Trough* and *Welfare Ranching* to name two—advocating for the removal of cattle from public lands. Those books show what a hell of a bargain the grazing fees are especially for smaller ranchers. Few of the occupiers had knowledge of how the refuge came to be, of the Paiute history of the area, or the terrible implication of what they were demanding and how it would negatively impact the very ones the protest was advocating for. "No one's the boss of me" could be their blunt-instrument-thinking mantra. With all due respect, the media were not overnight authorities on these subjects either, and the result was the spread of a lot of misinformation about the management of America's public lands and of the occupiers as symbols of the ranching West. Aided by traditional and social media, repetition is ever more powerful than truth and, from a safe virtual distance, makes it all too easy to fan the flames of hate.

Privatizing federal lands in the high desert, as Bundy demanded, would ultimately mean only one thing: big money would come in, swoop up the land, restrict all recreational access (including hunting), control waterways, and in so doing, send small ranchers and farmers down the river. Herring posits that wide-scale privatization would transform the United States as we know it.

> Federal water rights that underpin entire agricultural economies, and that are critical to some of the last family farms and ranches in America, will be in play. Few Americans, even those in the cities of the East who know nothing about these lands, will be untouched by the transformation. Once the precedent for divesting federal lands is well set, the Eastern public lands, most of them far more valuable than those in the West, will go on the international auction block. The unique American experiment in balancing public freedom and good with private interests will be forever shattered, while a new kind of inequality soars, not just inequality of economics and economic opportunity, but of life experience, the chance to experience liberty itself. The understanding that we all share something of value in common—the vast American landscape, yawning to all horizons and breathtakingly beautiful—will be further broken.

American plutocrats can't wait; they are salivating at the idea. The rest of us, including and especially the Ammon Bundys of the world, should oppose it with every ounce of our strength.

But if revolution is required to achieve change, Bundy succeeded. He flouted the law. He trespassed. He possessed and wielded weapons illegally. He vandalized federal property. Federal officials put the figure at $6 million in damages and other costs that were caused by the occupiers. He did all the things that revolutionaries do. And he got off easy, only twenty-two months in prison.

Apparently, taking the law into your own hands is acceptable if you're mistaken for the symbol of white America's cowboy culture. Speaking of getting off easy, get this: The occupiers were allowed to come and go in and out of the refuge during the occupation to, I don't know, get groceries, go to the laundromat, without being arrested even though what they were doing was against the law. County law enforcement was understandably trying its best not to poke the beast, to achieve a peaceful solution. Raise your hand if you think the same hall pass would have been given to non-white occupiers?

Certainly, many ranchers felt the occupation was the wrong tactic and did not subscribe to how they were being represented by the Bundy group. "It fills me with rage to define this region with the Bundy occupation," says rancher Becky Hyde. But many agreed it was the right fight. Jesse Laird, a rancher in the Warner Valley of Lake County, agreed with Bundy, according to a 2018 *Oregon Business* article, but not with his methods. "I felt like the way they went about it was wrong. They should have gone on a speaking tour." Many had been waiting a long time for a conversation with government land management agencies in which they felt heard. Maybe this is what they thought it required to achieve that end. But what ensued was very different and much bigger and more dangerous than anyone anticipated.

In the desert when the land gets stressed by drought or the soil disturbed, long-dormant weeds (read, issues of disenfranchisement, poverty) see their chance, suddenly erupt, take over. The Bundy occupation was like biting down on a broken tooth. It activated a national nerve. In a blink the small band camped in the middle of nowhere in Harney County, Oregon, protesting land-use laws became about too much government and opened fumaroles of hate and racism. Many blue-collar and middle-class workers, frustrated by diminishing returns, feeling unheard, unseen, unwitnessed, feeling that the language of those governing did not represent them, jumped on board. The occupation gave disgruntled whites a donkey to pin their issue on.

Hindsight being twenty-twenty, it's easy to track this slow boil of discontent in the high desert. The Sagebrush Rebellion of the 1970s and '80s protested what was called "federal colonialism" in the form of new environmental laws, especially the Federal Land Policy Management Act passed in 1976 that shifted the role of the BLM from maximizing extraction to preserving BLM lands. Landowners freaked out. In a January 2016 article that pieced together unrest in the West over the years, *High Country News* senior editor Jonathan Thompson came across this quote from then Colorado governor Richard Lamm on the subject of the rebellion:

[The] Sagebrush [Rebellion] comes into relief as what it really
is—a murky fusion of idealism and greed that may not be heroic,
nor righteous, nor even intelligent. Only one certainty exists—
that Sagebrush is a revolt against federal authority, and that its
taproot grows deep in the century's history. Beyond this, it is inco-
herent. Part hypocrisy, part demagoguery, partly the honest anger
of honest people, it is a movement of confusion and hysteria and
terrifyingly destructive potential. What it is no one fully understands.
What it will do no one can tell.

In his book *The Angry West*, Lamm further underscores the short-sightedness of the protest: "The proud West becomes the foolish

West. Worse, by continuing to act today as though it still has no need for the federal government, even as it continues to profit from federal largesse, it compounds its hypocrisy and undermines its credibility." This is especially true, whether it's good policy or not, in view of the fact, as Thompson points out, "hard rock miners have nearly unfettered access to federal lands and have to pay no royalties for the minerals they extract. Oil and gas drillers pay low royalties, and ranchers get a prime deal for grazing on BLM lands—royalties and grazing fees for state lands can be 50 percent higher or more than for federal lands."

But this was no time for logic or reason. The Bundy occupation was part of a perfect storm. Timing is everything. It activated every underserved white man's dormant frustration. It quickly bust through the region-centric issues of the Great Basin and marched across the nation. It provided a focus for rebels without a well-articulated cause who harbored hatred as a matter of principle. In the aftermath of the occupation, Oregon patriot and militia groups such as the Patriot Network, Three Percenters, and Oath Keepers felt emboldened, showed up as candidates on county ballots, flew Confederate flags from the beds of their pickups, and slapped "Oregunian" bumper stickers on their fenders. "We have become inured to fact that we live in a gun culture," says documentary filmmaker Richard Wilhelm, whose film *Refuge*, about the occupation, premiered in 2020.

At the trials for the occupation cohort, the government rolled into the courtroom carts piled high with weapons of all sorts and buckets of spent ammo casings. The result the government had intended, that the jury would be emotionally influenced by all the armament and, therefore, reject the defendants' defense, was a lead balloon (pardon the pun). Watching the jury, we noticed there were more than a few that seemed to like what they saw, and they'd like to own a few of the guns themselves to add to their collections. Again, it's the acceptance and understanding of a 'foreign' culture that is critical to our ability to move forward in this world. The government had a very difficult path toward conviction, and they came up short.

The windows of the false-fronted Paulina, Oregon, store used to display invitations to the monthly Pau Mau (Paulina-Maury Mountains) meetings of local ranch women, dances at the community hall, Paulina School events, but now a large sign takes up the window: WE WILL NOT COMPLY WITH GUN LAW CHANGES. Venture inside and you can get your coffee mug refilled with anger and resentment at no extra charge. National-level groups such as the Coalition of Western States, the Freedom Foundation, and the American Legislative Exchange Council adopted the occupation to fan the flames of their extreme efforts to privatize everything. Spoiling for a fight, they have ushered in a highly uncivil civil war.

Is war, conflict, combat, bloodshed the only way? Botanist and environmentalist Stuart Garrett references Newton's third law of thermo dynamics: "For every action, there is an equal, opposite reaction. If the Bundys are on one side, then opposition has to have a strong reaction counteracting them. If the other side is reasonable, then conservationists will be reasonable." Essentially, an eye for an eye. Can different goals and objectives be accomplished without a fight? What is "the good fight"? For that matter, what do I know of fighting, of war, of believing something so strongly that I take a public stand? Of laying my life down for a cause? What do I know of that sort of commitment?

✦

My generation's war was Vietnam. I was, at best, a dilettante pro-
tester, selective marcher, could sound smart about Allard Lowen-
stein's success in turning anti-war protest into a mainstream cause,
but didn't actively volunteer for Americans for Democratic Action. I
could claim some knowledge of the bumpy history of the Students
for a Democratic Society but never joined. I was more of a bystander,
entertained by the creative solutions some of my friends adopted to
avoid being drafted—feigning bad eyesight or bad backs, or escaping
to Canada.

In paradoxical juxtaposition to another war of that time, the
women's liberation movement, as a female I profited from the Vietnam War. As young male draftees were shipped away to fight after
college, I shipped off to Africa, having received a travel and study
fellowship previously only offered to male candidates. The fellowship didn't provide qualifying men exemption from the draft, so the
opportunity was reluctantly opened to women. Being in Ethiopia
and Madagascar in those days, the early '70s, meant you were truly
far away—to talk with anyone in the United States was done through
ham radio, letters took forever. I was now even further removed from
what was taking place in the United States as war protests escalated
along with the war itself.

It's still true of the upper country of the high desert—when some
note- or gossip-worthy development or occurrence takes place, word
travels fast between the far-flung ranches aided, in those days, by party
lines, brandings, meetings of women's club, community team rop-
ings, or chance encounters between pickups along the miles of dirt
roads that laced through the sage-covered reaches of the country—
one rancher lowering his window, sending a stream of brown tobacco

juice to the ground while taking in the latest news delivered by his neighbor. Even by upper-country standards, where any manner of unusual tales unfold, this was a doozy.

December of 1975. Word was that a Vietnamese family had been moved into an isolated cabin near Post, Oregon, to work on an adjacent ranch. A young couple with one, two, three kids. It made no sense. It was the dead of a serious winter. Speculation. Rumor. The owner? Absentee. Living in California. Were there cattle to feed? No one seemed to think so. Maybe. Whaddya make of it? Damned if I know. Didn't he have a local buckaroo feeding the cattle? Gonna need firewood. Damn straight. What is there for them to do? Nothing much, not this time of year.

That was true. By December most cow-calf operators in the high desert had already sold that year's crop of calves. Mother cows had been pregnancy checked. Culls—cows that came up "dry," hadn't bred back—had been sold. Bulls were sidelined, dismissed until after the cows calved the next spring, relegated to a separate pasture. They stood around all day, kind of broody and useless looking. All but one of the cavvy of ranch horses turned out until spring. The summer wranglers and the hay crew had long since left. In our high-desert ranch house it was only my husband, me, and our toddler at the dinner table, and outside the pristine silence of the winter desert, the sallow moon illuminating an infinity pool of white snow that fell away at the dark edge of the night. It was the one time of year ranchers could take some time away. Reno, Las Vegas, Mexico. The hired man could keep the water troughs open, do the feeding—put the pickup in low gear and let it hobble across the hardpan fields while he tossed hay bales off the back to the line of waiting cows.

So it was reasonable to question why a couple had been hired this time of year. And from Vietnam, of all things. I was determined to find an answer albeit for embarrassingly self-serving and naïve reasons (I thought I could bone up on my French with them). On my way into Prineville to do errands I'd stop at the Post store for directions to their cabin. It turned out to be the right action for the wrong reasons. Funny how that works. I left our ranch early that morning, armed with the usual long list of things to do: groceries, salt licks and supplement for the cows, grain for the horses, and a doctor's appointment. "Your turn for a preg check," my husband said, jokingly referring to the annual check given to our (hopefully) bred mother cows.

To understand how a family from Vietnam could have possibly wound up in Post, Oregon, meant delving deeper into my generation's war. It turned out there was an explanation. Goes like this. After ten years of protests in the United States and terrible bloodshed in Vietnam, in 1973 the Paris Peace Accords were signed and the last of the US troops left Saigon despite the fact that fighting between the North and South Vietnamese persisted. The South, cut off at the knees by the US departure, was unable to defend against an offensive by the North Vietnamese, resulting in the fall of Saigon. As the North Vietnamese closed in on the capital, a massive helicopter evacuation was staged. The last whirlybird took off from Saigon on April 30, 1975. The pro-American South Vietnamese civilians left behind swarmed the shores in hopes of fleeing the country by sea. One hundred thousand lucky boat people, as they came to be called, managed to reach US military ships moored off the coast and were taken aboard.

Meanwhile the International Rescue Committee scrambled to set up refugee camps in the United States and other Southeast Asian countries. Military bases became processing centers. The priority was to find, as quickly and efficiently as possible, sponsors, housing, and jobs for the refugees. To speed the process along, government grants of $500 per refugee were offered to private settlement efforts. Place a family of four: $2,000. Ten families of that size: $20,000. Starts to be a good business proposition. Good things happened but so did greed and graft. Some created fictitious businesses and left families stranded with no resources or understanding where they were or what they were to do.

On my way to town, I navigated miles of roads covered with snow so light it billowed behind my car like white dust. I reached the plowed paved road and turned toward Post. The banks of the Crooked River were saw-toothed with brittle fingers of ice reaching into the river. Ryegrass, teasel, and the nose hairs of the cattle were lined with frost. Steam rose off the water that still moved. It was cold.

I got to Post and inquired inside the general store. The owner cocked her head to the west, in the direction of a dirt road that led away from the store toward the river. I got back in my car and drove down the road she had indicated, eventually pulling up in front of a small, primitive cabin. Smoke steamed out of a rusty metal chimney pipe. I knocked.

Opening the door only a crack, a tiny young woman with a cap of jet-black hair peered out. I announced my name. The door was abruptly closed. Inside there was a lot of rapid conversation in Vietnamese. I waited. Then the door was opened slowly. I said hello again in English and French, said my name pointing at myself, ridiculously holding up my English/French dictionary, this time to a man, young and lean, who eyed me suspiciously, then cautiously gestured me inside. The cabin had a single bed, a woodstove, a table. The few kitchen utensils were arranged carefully and precisely on the table: knives, spatula, a pot, a few plates. A toddler was tucked in the bed, the young woman, now seated at the table, held a baby to her breast.

Suddenly a torrent of words, gestures from her husband. Opening empty cupboards. Patting his stomach. Rubbing his forearms to indicate how cold he was. He included his wife and children in his pantomime. I too resorted to improvised sign language. *I would drive* I mimed turning a steering wheel, *talk* I mimed talking on a telephone, *would bring to them*. After my solo pantomime they seemed to understand I was concerned and would help them. Amid excited chatter on their part, we exchanged names. I also wrote down my phone number, not that they had a phone but there was one at the Post store. Only what would we have been able to say to one another? They passed the slip of paper back and forth as though it was a visa to heaven, tracing my writing with their fingers. They rehearsed my name over and over, running my first name and last initial together into one. "EllieB, EllieB, EllieB."

My list of errands to do in town had just grown a lot longer. What unfolded was nothing short of a fast-acting miracle produced by a small army of people in Prineville united by caring and compassion. I had little to do with it, had only to blow on the pilot light of concern, make a few calls once I got to town, and within days, a house was obtained, and a former Marine who spoke Vietnamese helped Mr. V. get a driver's license and a job at the lumber mill. I, amid all this, delivered my second child and returned to ranching. Telephone conversations over the next few weeks confirmed that clothing, household supplies, and a car had been donated.

Piecing their story together, this is what I came up with. Mr. V., formerly a farmer, had worked for the American military and was in significant danger when Saigon was overtaken by the North Vietnamese. He, his pregnant wife, and their firstborn managed to get on a cargo ship and were delivered to Guam, where their second child was born. They were then transported to Camp Pendleton in

California, joining thousands of refugees there. At first, according to reports, refugees were allowed to turn down sponsor offers if the climate at the proposed relocation site was deemed too cold or it meant separating family members or the work was unfamiliar. But to speed things up, the American government under President Gerald Ford decided to allow only two sponsorship declines and then they had to accept. According to the stories making their way up and down the Crooked River valley, the ranch owner had created a landscape company in California placing numbers of families. Did he end up with one extra family? Have to stick them somewhere, so sent them to his ranch in Oregon? Whatever had brought them to Post, a second relocation effort took shape, this time not across the Pacific but across a sagebrush ocean, this time not on a cargo ship but within the hold of a warmhearted group of central Oregonians. This time a much shorter distance—from Post to Prineville, Oregon.

I eventually moved away from the Prineville area. It would not be until the summer of 2010, recalling this family and determined to reconnect on the thirty-fifth anniversary of the evacuation of Saigon, that we would reunite. We met at a Chinese restaurant in Prineville. They weren't happy about my disappearance. They said they wondered where I had gone and had looked for me, tried to call, but they couldn't find my name in the phone book. (My efforts to explain that I had returned to my maiden name were lost on them.) They said they had worried about me and wondered if I was still their friend. After I assured them we were, they shared stories of receiving citizenship, working, fishing. All five of their children have finished school. The youngest is becoming a doctor. Though Mr. V. drives the same car obtained for him way back then, he proudly stated he had purchased a car and a computer for each of his children. The one luxury he permits himself, a satellite television package so he can watch the news of Vietnam in Vietnamese. He and his wife have worked hard for what all of us want—to create a better life for our children. They talk to me of their dreams of retiring, getting a camper, and traveling the United States. We all nod in enthusiastic agreement to what fun that would be.

I let them know I must be going. Mr. V. walks with me to my car talking a blue but heavily accented streak. I watch a young, white, twenty-something Prineville youth walk by, his jeans slung low. What was that look? Dislike? Disdain? Distrust? Worse? Fired by the rhetoric of anti-immigrant newscasts and political candidates, by messages of intolerance and fear, what can small-town youth be expected to know of compassion, of Washington State's OneAmerica, as India-born US congresswoman Pramila Jayapal advocates?

Visiting the Oregon Coast recently, I decided to indulge myself with a manicure. I looked in the Yellow Pages and randomly picked a salon, making an appointment at B Nail. I found the location in the shopping mall at the entrance to town. I walked in. Two Vietnamese women in surgical masks sat at small tables working silently, purposefully on the hands or feet of their female clients, gesturing them to place their foot in the wash basin, their hand in the fluted finger bowl. A metallic portrait of the Buddha was hung on one wall. On the opposite wall, a painting of very stylized white horses rearing into purple and pink clouds. I was directed to a young Vietnamese man. Sitting down across a narrow table from him, I placed my hands, palms down, like some sort of supplicant, on a white hand towel. He examined each finger, one by one, picking them up and dropping them like playing the reeds of a kalimba. He then went to work shaping my nails, turning my hand in his palm this way and that with professional dispatch as though fileting a fish or shaping dough, finally applying scarlet polish on each nail. Two brown-eyed children stuck their heads in the door at the rear of the storefront. He said something in Vietnamese that sent them obediently back, closing the door quietly behind them. "Your daughters?" "Yes." "Back from school?" "Yes." "Good students?" "Yes. Very good. Very good." He smiled. I smiled.

There we sat, across from one another, my old hand supported in his young palm—mismatched in size, age, color yet joined in some sort of inadvertent, circumstantial prayer or arrested applause. I was startled by the sudden sensation that our life stories were being transmitted one hand to the other through a palpable current of shared compassion for whatever arc of history and story brought him here, whatever arc of history and story brought me here, what of war he had heard from his parents, his grandparents, what hardships we had both, any of us everywhere, endured, what triumphs. My hand floating in his palm, I felt hope that we are all up to the ultimate and critical relocation that beckons—from a divided America, a divided globe, to a unified and tolerant one. Raising the tiny red lacquer-soaked brush in the air like a conductor, he asked for my other hand.

This is not so much a story of what I know of war. More, it addresses what I have witnessed of the instinct for peacemaking, of mutual respect, the desire to make possibility and opportunity the scaffolding for the American Dream. It's my idea of demilitarization. In view of what the family from Vietnam was escaping, what migrants from Central America or the Middle East are escaping, what our ancestors were escaping when they arrived on the shores of the United States, shame on us as a country if we deny them the opportunity to thrive.

✦

For most, regardless of political perspective, the initial reaction to the Bundy occupation was that it couldn't possibly last. But as it dragged on, as the media hype increased, emboldening the occupiers, those who wanted their town back or who had ties to the refuge, from hunters to birders, felt personally robbed of access to a national treasure. And they said so. People gathered to march down the main street of Burns, separating to either side of the street depending on whether they were for or against the occupation. Julie Weikel, a member of the Wild Horse and Burro Commission, a former ONDA board member, and a retired veterinarian who lives in Princeton, Oregon, near the refuge, spotted her neighbor standing on the pro-Bundy side of the road, and with her trademark chutzpah and humor yelled, "Get over here!" Alice Elshoff and the central Oregon chapter of the Great Old Broads for Wilderness organized a protest in Bend; the women wore aprons and wielded rolling pins, telling the occupiers to go back "to your mamas," putting into perspective all the hoopla the occupation had garnered.

The occupiers were like something out of central casting, a ragged band of misfits. Make that *type*casting and we are all guilty, based on how simplistically we typed them, with us or agin us, radical or reasonable, rich or poor, smart or not. Look deep enough and aspects of each of us were represented—in the family escaping Vietnam or in the group gathered around the campfire at the refuge. Find your story in their story. Know that we are all one story.

✦

The Malheur occupation took place in January. What had manifested as a Brownian movement of white dissent across the country, including the Sagebrush Rebellion, became focused and, as fate would have it, found a powerful spokesperson. It was none of those around the refuge campfire. The anger and resentment it brought to the surface played into a much bigger event: the presidential election in November of that year.

The ultimate winner built a base for his campaign on the backs of frustrated middle- and lower-class whites. He stirred up their latent frustration predicated on an old and scary tactic. In the United States the wealthiest whites have, since settlers first arrived, relied on the allegiance and support of underclass whites to maintain their position at the top of the food chain. They forged that allegiance by pitting working white people against people of color. Like hawkers of land during the homesteading years in the West, the language is slick, sensational. To use a favorite ranchism, they are "pie crust promises, easily made, easily broken." The winner of the 2016 presidential election has proved to be self-serving and corrupt, one who made a practice of fueling false hopes among his base that their lives can and will be improved, but only at the expense of other minorities. It has never worked out. The aftermath of the honeymoon on the part of whites, still underemployed and sidelined, is only more vitriol and rage. But so deviously clever is this scheme that the victimized base takes it out not on the perpetrator of the story, as they should, but on the targeted minorities. This manipulation of class and color is traced back to plantation owners as slavery ended, according to an article by Jonna Ivin titled "I Know Why Poor Whites Chant Trump, Trump, Trump." She maintains that the landholders feared that poor whites would unite with blacks after the end of slavery and overwhelm the wealthy white elites' fragile perch at the top, so the strategy was to create division by spreading fear. The soon-to-be-freed black slaves were cast as the enemy of lower-class whites.

Black men raping white women. The enemy as "other." The "other" as Godless.

The updated version of this story has changed the exclusive focus on blacks to all people of color, most notably migrants crossing the southern border of the United States who are cast as thugs, rapists, drug dealers, terrorists, and heathens. Racism, in support of a small group maintaining their privileges of power, is once again being used as a means of oppression.

But what his base fails to see is that they are as much the victim of this tactic as any minority. Martin Luther King Jr., put behind bars for protesting, asked the white jail-keepers how much they were paid. King recalls what happened next in one of his most famous sermons, "The Drum Major Instinct." "I said 'Now you know what? You ought to be marching with us. You're just as poor as Negroes. . . . You fail to see that the same forces that oppress Negroes in American society oppress poor white people."

Ivin says, regardless of color or religious belief, all poor are bona fide members of the same class: the poor. They are "all sides of the same coin, a coin that has been held in the pocket of the elite class since the first settlers arrived in the American colonies."

"I am no one special," says Ivin, who herself has experienced extreme poverty.

I am a poor, uneducated, white woman. I am the white under-class, and I am no one's enemy. I fight for racial equality because people of color are not my enemy. Gays, lesbians, bisexuals, and transgender people are not my enemy. Immigrants and refugees are not my enemy. Muslims are not my enemy. Native Americans are not my enemy. Single mothers and fathers are not my enemy. People on Medicare, disability, food stamps, and unemployment

are not my enemy. The homeless are not my enemy. . . . Other
people are not the enemy, no matter how they look, how they pray,
or who they love. They are fighting to be heard. They are people
who . . . agree with the statement, "People like me don't have any
say about what government does."

Many pooh-poohed the notion that the Malheur occupation would
last or amount to anything, but it gave voice to a deep-seated sense
of being second-class citizens, of a hopelessness felt by struggling
middle-class and poor white families. To paraphrase the band Sawyer
Brown, I may not be first class, but I'm sure as heck not white trash.

We are all complicit in this to greater and lesser degrees. Most of
us want to follow the rules, want to do the right thing, don't want to
rock the boat of employment and family security. Few of us, it turns
out, are trailblazers. Most are willing to have an adventure, sure, but
a handheld adventure. Most of us like to color, albeit wildly, inside
lines someone else has drawn. That may be, in an oblique way, good
news for the preservation of open and wild spaces. But in the larger
sense this compliance, this low-grade passivity has put entire nations
into a trance, one group following a grim reaper for whom his or
her "followers" have no value, the other trying to behave themselves
so they can have a life, ignoring the warning signs. Omelas redux.
A nation of sleepwalkers.

It may seem we're a long way off the trail. We're not. Every step
taken by a hiker on the Oregon Desert Trail is a vote against privatization and for conservation. Lift all restrictions on environmental protection? Guess who wins. Privatization of public lands? It means only
one thing: more for the wealthy elite and inaccessibility for the majority of us. When small, privately held ranchers turn out on BLM, their
needs must be protected in concert with the goals of environmental

and conservation groups. The more "y'all come" we can be, the more success is likely. Ranchers and environmentalists and the BLM have been trying for decades to get it right, and though it hasn't always been graceful, it is an ongoing dialogue. If easy, it would have been accomplished. It is a sliding baseline with different demands to accommodate almost daily. Good solutions take time with so many working parts and demands. A different kind of civil war is called for—a war of civility, mutual respect, consensus, crossing aisles.

I have made it to the top of Steens Mountain. I step up to the gnarled juniper lectern, grasp the old limbs, lean into the sage-scented breeze, listen to rocks tumble down, down the steep face, loosed by fleeing mountain sheep, nimble over the basalt cliffs and ledges. I plant a small flag of promise to myself as I look out over the Alvord Desert below. How I love this big country. What affection I have for the people who live here. From them I have learned hard work, honesty, how to show up, improvisation, making do, neighbors helping neighbors, community, giving, joy. I run pell-mell down Wildhorse Canyon, tumbling toward a treeless, vast flat expanse, another definition of eternity as expressed by the Alvord Desert. Hot springs ooze and belch. The molten center of the earth beckons. The landscape is like something out of the bizarre world Ingmar Bergman created in his films. And what's that? On that flatbed? It looks like a grand piano wrapped in bubble wrap on a mattress.

Your eyes do not deceive. Plan it right and you could be getting to the Alvord Desert in time for a classical piano concert. Yes, you heard me right. I'm talking Hunter Noack, the creative genius and classical pianist who hauls his Steinway concert grand piano around on a trailer, parking it in the most remote locations in Oregon during the summer to perform free concerts. Noack embodies the kind of out-of-the-box thinking and imagination that forces us to look at our petty shit for what it is, at divisions and conflicts for the waste of time they are. With his nimble fingers, Noack reads the dusty Braille of the keys, unveils our suffering, soothes this rocky world's sharps and flats, repairs the frayed cords of kindness. He scales the ineffable longing we have for love summoned by ghost notes and fugues. He dares us to jump backward off the edge of everything, rappelling note by descending note to land where we all began as stardust, a single cell, in the desert. The language of classical music as the ultimate peace pipe. He calls the series "In a Landscape: Classical Music in the Wild." People emerge out of the gloaming for the concert in the Alvord. Camp chairs are set up, picnics spread out on blankets. The Steinway is unwrapped, tuned. Earphones are available that remotely transmit the concert directly to your picnic chair or you can listen plein air, watch the notes rise, gather, and be swept away by the desert's evening breeze.

OWYHEE CANYONLANDS

At the top [of Louse Canyon] a cowboy and his son rode upon me seemingly out of nowhere. They were fetching cattle. . . . We spoke of land ethics, a common topic when lonesome strangers encounter each other in the big vistas. Clearly, we came from different political views, however . . . we shared a common ground on land ethics. I had been the first overland hiker he had seen in his lifetime out there in the Owyhee Desert. And in earnest I could see how much he cared for the land . . . we all need places to go, to use, but we need all of each other connected. A coyote appeared traipsing a short distance away, not leaning one way or the other, simply wandering the land unoccupied, an opportunist trying to seam together rifts while going unnoticed.

THRU-HIKER RYAN "DIRTMONGER" SYLVA

FOURTEEN

All Roads Lead to Rome

T HE TRAIL HAS hopscotched from one wilderness study area
to another, one tract of BLM to another, one US Forest Service
allotment to another, an allemande of the many long-established
land conservation successes as well as new ones currently underway.
The final stretch through the dramatic Pillars of Rome and the
Owyhee Canyonlands is coming up, the most rugged and challenging portion of the trek and, in terms of geologic drama and scale, the
most beautiful.

This is not to take anything away from the steep descent off
Steens Mountain nor the intense heat and winds while traversing
the pancake-flat, desiccated Alvord Desert after Hunter Noack's concert. If you're lucky, the dizzying monotony of the seven-mile-wide,
twelve-mile-long ancient lakebed is sometimes relieved by the "Go
figure!" sight of a land yacht jetting past on its splayed tricycle construction. It whistles and rattles as the goggled Red Baron at the
helm converts five miles per hour wind into fifty miles per hour land

speed, curses "sucker puffs" that lure sailors halfway across the flats only to drop them, forcing them to push the praying mantis of a contraption back to their camp. ODT hikers walk, of course, but also traverse portions on horseback, on mountain bikes, in kayaks or, to ford a river, by backpack swimming. In fact, the detailed guide to the trail produced by Renee Patrick of the Oregon Natural Desert Association gives suggestions as to when you can best get off your feet while still ticking off the miles. So far none have enlisted a sand yacht or dirt boat, as they are also called.

Another Alvord distraction is the Alvord Hot Springs, complete with campground and adequate bathroom facilities and a hot dip in any number of thermal springs in open-air pools or enclosed in weathered shacks. Trekkers will likely spot the remains of sod huts near ten-acre Borax Lake's hot springs, all that's left of the primitive housing provided to Chinese laborers who mined the mineral starting in the late nineteenth through the mid-twentieth century. The element boron's presence on earth is the result of the blasts of supernovae taking place at a safe distance from earth and making earthfall in the form of boron stardust, giving "star material" new meaning. At its peak, the Alvord borax works could produce five tons a day. The large, rusted-out vats that litter the desert once stored the boron-rich water that was treated with acid, boiled, using sagebrush as fuel, then cooled. The crystallized stardust was hauled by mule teams to the nearest rail spur in Winnemucca, Nevada, 130 miles away. The Twenty Mule Team Borax brand of cleanser, still sold today, is named after these hardworking teams. The vats littering the high desert are a reminder of the mining and mineral extractions that have taken place, are taking place, and are proposed in the high desert, across the West, and throughout the world. What is the cost to the environment and to those who mine these buried treasures?

Leaving the Alvord, the tiny outpost of Fields is the only bastion of civilization, loosely defined, between Denio, twenty-two miles to the south, and Frenchglen, fifty to the north. And unless a hiker detours into Denio, Nevada, for a shower and food before taking on the Trout Creek and Pueblo Mountains on Oregon's southern border, Fields is the last opportunity for restocking before the whistle-stop of Rome on the Owyhee River. It's there trekkers take a deep breath before undertaking the homestretch through the canyonlands. The Fields store, which includes a café, gas station, hotel, and post office all operated by the same family, is a watering hole for area ranchers and cowboys and a stopping point for tourists visiting the area.

It's also the nearest store for John Simpkins, a visual artist who lives in the ghost town of Andrews, fifteen miles north. His paintings are dreamlike and prophetic, contemporary and timeless. His highly stylized imagery is rooted in American primitivism and folkloric traditions and rendered in a one-dimensional, flat-screened, Russian icon style. With no dominant perspective, he simultaneously creates multiple perspectives, something we could all stand to do. He turns the world and our view of it inside out.

When my children were young, I volunteered as a 4-H leader in photography for some of the neighboring ranch kids. I worked as a photographer before I was married, so it was familiar territory. We called our club the Snapshooters. Their display of homemade cameras and the images taken with them won a blue ribbon at the county fair that year. They made pinhole cameras out of variously shaped boxes and painted the insides with flat, black paint. They then cut a small square out of one end and covered it with a piece of tinfoil taped down on all sides. Next, they surgically pierced the center of the tinfoil with a straight pin, and finally, folding a piece of tape back on itself, made a lens cover to keep the light out of the inside of the box until they were ready to take a picture. We fashioned a darkroom in the closet of the feedlot scale house where I daily dispatched feed and cattle trucks. All eight in the club, ranging in age from four to twelve, squeezed inside the small room. They were giddy with the intrigue and mystery of being backstage in a darkened theater just before the curtain goes up. Around the doorframe we placed rolled-up bath towels that we secured with black tape. The yellow safelight was turned off, and each box loaded with a single sheet of light-sensitive paper. The children, now adapted to the darkness, then taped the lids of their boxes down, so no light could leak in.

Once everyone was ready, we opened the door, our eyes blinded by the sudden rush of daylight, and ran outside. It was almost impossible to accurately aim the cameras. But they thought they could, propping their boxes on the side of a rock or on a discarded tire and then lying down on the ground to better aim their pinhole camera, like a golfer lining up a difficult putt. They pulled off the lens cap, counted one one thousand up to ten as we had rehearsed, and then resealed the pinhole with the piece of tape and hurried back to the darkroom. In their imaginations they pictured their final product—the entire alfalfa field that lay below the feed pens, a magpie flying by, the lone heifer in the corral.

In the darkroom, as the images slowly emerged in the tray of developer, it took them a while to figure out what they had, in fact, photographed. It was a colorless and negative image. What was light was dark, and dark light. Maybe the sharp edge of the corral with the head of the heifer only just visible; maybe the phone pole, instead of the magpie flying by; maybe the harrow in the foreground, instead of the alfalfa field. Though the photograph wasn't what they had thought it would be, they weren't disappointed. That a camera they built out of a box plus a special piece of paper captured an image was magic to them. And then there was the funny thing of it being a negative one, inside out and upside down. I talked to them about light and dark, how light affected the surface of the paper.

Looking at the results of the day's labor—wet sheets of printing paper hanging like a string of fish from clothespins on a line suspended across the makeshift darkroom—I could see in their young faces a kind of beyondness, an otherness as it struck them that what they thought they saw wasn't all there was to see, what they thought they knew wasn't all there was to know. Light or lack of, color or lack of, perspective or lack of altered their emerging sense of reality.

So it is with John Simpkins's work. Simpkins landed in Andrews, Oregon, thanks to George Stroemple, an internationally recognized art collector based in Portland, a strong advocate of Simpkins's art, and as fate would have it, a property owner in Andrews. Grief-stricken after his partner, Victor Brumbach, died, Simpkins sold everything and carried some of Brumbach's ashes to Tibet, to the sacred Lhamo La-tso Lake situated in the Himalayas. Struck by the beauty and wildness of the place, Simpkins made the wish that he would find somewhere in the United States that looked like that. Stroemple had just the thing. "The moment I turned at the triangle down by Fields— what they call Long Hollow—I made that turn and faced north toward the Steens up here at Wild Horse Canyon, and I knew," Simpkins said in an article in Bend's *1859* magazine. "I saw that and I knew that I had gotten my wish."

He moved to Andrews in 2011, lives in the teacherage, and uses the nearby schoolhouse as his studio. The space inside and the space outside have inspired him to tackle much larger canvases than he did earlier in his career. "My contact [with the world] really began to solidify with the earth itself," he said.

Safe to say that ranchers and cowboys that come to Fields for their mail, a school function, fuel, or groceries initially didn't know what to make of this artist, this mystic, this loner living down the road, this changer of perspectives. I heard he was recently paid a high compliment by local standards, given a pass into the brotherhood of the region, when a visitor asked a pistol-packing employee at the Fields store about Simpkins. "Well, he ain't dead yet."

After Fields, the ODT heads counterintuitively south into the beautiful basins and ridges of the Pueblo Mountains. It is *counterintuitively* if the shortest distance between two points is a straight line, but that is not the way of the ODT. No, staying on public ground means zigs and zags, so to go north and east you go south. Thruhiker Mary "Fireweed" Kwart reminds us that there is an ODT map for the Pueblos locating the cairns "that lead you from summit to summit traversing the range." Heather "Anish" Anderson chimes in: "The Pueblos were a delightful surprise. This mountain range is tucked along the Oregon/Nevada border and travel was nearly entirely cross-country. Bighorn sheep were abundant. The descent to Denio Canyon was some of the thickest bushwhacking I have ever done in a narrow canyon with water rushing through." Credit for this section of the trail, from the Steens to the Alvord and over to the Pueblos, goes to the Desert Trail Association (DTA), started in 1960 by the late Russ Pengelly, who taught biology in Burns, Oregon. At the time the Pueblos were virtually unknown (now everything is "virtually" known). Terry Richard of the *Oregonian* noted then that the Pueblos "were so little-known . . . the mountain range could well have been on the surface of Mars." The goal of the DTA was a two-thousand-mile hiking route from Mexico to the Continental Divide

Trail in Idaho and on to Canada, which was accomplished. ODT's own "Dirtmonger" was only the second person to hike it, a feat he accomplished in 2018. Though now on life support as an organization, the Desert Trail Association's Pueblo and Steens Mountain sections were each designated as a National Recreation Trail and are included on ODT trail maps.

Danny "Caribou" Archibald, after traversing the Pueblos, decided to detour into Nevada after a day he described in a breathless voice-over on his GoPro video: "Only on the ODT is it sleeting and blue sky and rain all at the same time. Like . . . this is a crazy place. Throwing everything at me. Wild. June 9 and it's snowing!" His video shows a close-up of angry heel blisters the size of plums. A night in Denio seemed a very good idea. After tending to his wounds and getting a good night's sleep, he documents his departure as he heads for the Trout Creek Mountains. His camera takes in the endless stretch of road ahead and then pans to the official "Welcome to Oregon" green highway sign as he crosses the state line. Someone had stuck a decal to the lower right corner: "Read a fucking book." Danny sprinted gleefully ahead. "I did not use technology for mapping," Danny explained to me.

I did use my phone to call people from time to time in towns. The purpose of my trip was divided. One, to see a part of the country I had never seen and to see what the desert was like. I also was working on a grant from my school studying identity and politics in the desert. And, because it makes me happy. A tip for other thru-hikers: Remember why you want to be where you are, and find tangible moments in your life that remind you of that reason. Some wonderful encounters with people throughout. From start to finish. Wonderful kindness and openness.

The Trout Creek Mountains, where Danny was headed, are far from everywhere, close to nothing, and not impressively high, at best only rising to arid plateau summits of eight thousand feet. These mountains don't get much press, especially after the headliners of Steens and Hart Mountains and the dramatic escarpments the ODT has traversed, but they are a good dress rehearsal for the Owyhee Canyonlands as Trout Creeks' rugged gorges make light of the rocky bluffs and buttes they cleave.

What *did* bring attention to the Trout Creek Mountains were challenges to grazing on public allotments in the face of demands for the protection of endangered species, rehabilitation of riparian zones, and claims of overstocking. At first the protests of environmentalists were noisily answered by the Sagebrush Rebellion, a line-in-the-sand response by ranchers against draconian grazing restrictions. But divisiveness gave way to the formation of the Trout Creek Mountain Working Group, which developed a new grazing allotment management plan in 1991 to protect both the land's ecological health and the ranchers' economic needs. Instead of fisticuffs between environmental interests, federal agencies, and ranchers, the Trout Creek Mountain Working Group painstakingly crafted another approach. The late, great rancher and visionary Doc Hatfield was quoted as saying, "If we can have economics and ecology without trampling property rights or compromising the BLM's obligations to the public, we've got it in the bag."

The Trout Creek Mountains are still recovering from the 2012 Holloway Fire that burned 460,000 aces. For hikers, Willow Creek Hot Springs, a small BLM campground, is a welcome green oasis, having escaped the worst of the inferno. It is just what the doctor ordered after a day's worth of desert dust.

No one needs to be reminded of the incidences of huge forest and grass fires in Oregon, California, Colorado, Washington, Arizona, and western Canada with mirror images raging in Australia and other parts of the world for the same reasons: human impact, climate change, extended periods of drought. As Wallace Stegner wrote, "We have acted upon the western landscape with the force of a geological agent." Recent studies from Portland State University show that, in the aftermath of a fire, snowmelt accelerates due to lack of cover and shade, so the problem self-exacerbates. Fires are now assumed during Oregon's summers, which are consistently hotter than ever before.

In 2018 Bend essentially got no rain between May and October. In a town where an air conditioner was never even considered, they are now de rigeur. Never mind the impact of fires, the snowpack in the Cascades is already diminishing more rapidly in direct proportion to the rising temperatures. Bend is listed as a high-risk candidate for a large forest fire due to insect infestations that thrive in the warmer winters. The Oregon Shakespeare Festival, a regional repertory theater founded in 1935 and located in Ashland, is west and far enough south of the ODT that its surrounding hills feature vineyards, orchards, and California scrub oak. Annually from March through October the festival stages classics, musicals, new works, and Shakespeare productions in two indoor performance spaces and in an open-air Elizabethan theater. In recent years, since the advent of "smoke" season, the thick haze from California fires has taken a sizable bite out of Ashland's estimated annual attendance of four hundred thousand. Sisters, Oregon, down the road from Bend, attracts worldwide talent and thousands of attendees to its annual three-day Labor Day weekend folk festival. It was abruptly canceled in 2017 due to heavy smoke from nearby fires, painting the town's tourism-based economy with red ink.

Some version of these blues is being sung anywhere there is heat, wildlands, and lack of precipitation. Real estate agents now factor in fire insurance costs and proximity to forested public land. Stop, drop, and roll. On the wetter side of the picture, the risk analytics firm Four Twenty Seven claims that more than 10 percent of real estate in the United States, with an estimated value of $130 billion, is located in high-risk areas due to sea level rise. We adapt rather than fix. I asked Bill Marlett what level of exhaustion, concern, hope, or hopelessness he experiences post-ONDA and regarding the work he is now doing in Baja California Sur. "I am resigned to the reality of abrupt climate chaos," he replied. "We jumped off a cliff and dream of a soft landing. In the meantime, we do what we can with the gift of time and nature that remains."

Before the final, dramatic movement of this ODT symphony through the Owyhee Canyonlands, hikers can refresh at the small community of Rome (population eighty-seven), and photograph the bizarre namesakes of this stage stop: hundred-foot-tall pillars rising out of nowhere, fossil-bearing gray clay monoliths, like enormous hoodoos, suggesting ruined temples of an ancient culture constructed by imagined giants of the desert.

From here hikers have a choice. Make your way on foot, as sixty-seven-year-old thru-hiker Mary "Fireweed" Kwart did: "The incredible toughness of hiking in the canyon—having to swim with my pack in pools to progress through the Little West Owyhee Canyon. The beauty was over the top, started suffering 'grandeur fatigue' [quote of Colin Fletcher from his hike end to end of the Grand Canyon in the early '60s]. Biggest scare: being charged by a bull in the bottom of the canyon—managed to jab it with my hiking pole and it retreated. It came out of nowhere from the brush. A total surprise."

Or you can make your way by raft or kayak. Rome is where flotillas put in for five days of rodeoing through the rapids of the wild and scenic Owyhee River to the takeout at Leslie Gulch. The trips are held in the early spring and are dependent on runoff, serving as a barometer of precipitation in this part of the West. I was wait-listed three years before all systems were a watery go in 2017. One of a wide variety of outings in the high desert offered by ONDA, it was well worth the wait, the river trip of a lifetime, a week spent negotiating heart-stopping rapids, camping beneath towering brick-red and golden rhyolite canyon walls, picnicking next to natural hot springs bubbling from riverbanks or gardens of petroglyphs, and hiking in the evenings high above the pristine ribbon of water.

From these vantage points, hikers or rafters are looking out over a truly unique geologic display in one of the nation's wildest and most isolated areas. Water and weather have eroded rock layers deposited eons ago, souvenirs of explosive eruptions by ill-tempered calderas linked to the Yellowstone hot spot, a string of large molten pools that started bubbling in southeastern Oregon sixteen million years ago and made a final display in Yellowstone six hundred thousand years ago. This trail of fire didn't scorch its way under the earth's surface, rather the North American plate inched along over the top of these hot molten beds. Lest you think this is all ancient Owyhee Canyonlands history, think again. The most recent volcanic activity in the Owyhee area was at the big lava field of Jordan Craters thirty-two hundred years ago. That is no time, geologically speaking, and is confirmation that the Owyhee area is still in its volcanic prime.

Because of and in addition to the startling geology of the area, several species of plants are found nowhere else on the earth, Owyhee clover and Packard's blazingstar among them. The other flora and fauna in the Canyonlands that trekkers have gotten to know along the ODT are also here, well protected within the canyons' castle walls. It's not all good news. One of the nation's wildest and most isolated areas isn't immune to the impact of guess who? Native vegetation has been compromised by grazing and the suppression of natural fire cycles. Asian cheatgrass, introduced in the 1800s, has aggressively colonized the high desert along with invasive Russian thistle, the tumbling tumbleweed so many associate with cowboy lore. But nevertheless, the Canyonlands represent two million acres of relatively intact ecosystems.

No surprise that the area is a hot topic among ranchers and conservationists as what's best for most is sorted out. Proposed as a monument in 2016, the Canyonlands got pushback from ranchers and locals, resulting in it being dropped from President Obama's list of new monuments. But there is now renewed interest. Committees have been reconvened that include prominent ranchers and conservationists. Tim Davies of the Friends of the Owyhee is one of many who has worked to bring all sides together. As Brent Fenty, executive director of the Oregon Desert Land Trust and formerly of ONDA, says, "This would be a national park anywhere else." And it may be getting closer. In 2019 Senators Ron Wyden and Jeff Merkley introduced the Malheur Community Empowerment for the Owyhee Act that would designate more than one million acres as wilderness and protect more than fourteen miles of the Owyhee River as wild and scenic. At the same time it would also protect grazing and land-use laws.

Whether by land or by water, arriving at the Oregon Desert Trail's end at Leslie Gulch, you are duly saluted and celebrated. In honor of your accomplishment, an anthem is played on the organ pipes of soaring golden rhyolite walls, tributes to the manic magma displays of fury the Yellowstone hot spot caldera produced sixteen million years ago. The spires and sandcastle-like turrets rival any cathedral Antoni Gaudí rendered in Spain. Joining in on the tribute to your trek are the thousand rock mouths scoured round by wind and water in the sheer welded tuff formations. More or less compacted in certain areas, the tuff is unevenly susceptible to the effects of weather, hence the honeycomb-like façade. Surrounded by rabbitbrush's flavescence, stop and listen to the wind blow "oooh" across their volcanic lips like so many Coke bottles, "oooh" they hum in unison, in merry appreciation of what you have accomplished. The celebration, high-desert style, ends with the soft advent of evening—chroma jazz, a closing riff of dark goldenrod notes in the gloaming.

And then it's done. The miles, the metaphors. The hiker sloughs his battered backpack and bedroll, finds friends waiting to drive her back to "civilization." The end of the trail. Sort of. Oregon Desert Trail wisdom has a way of clinging to socks like cheatgrass, to hearts like glitter. To know the end is to know the beginning. To know the end is to embrace life. The footstep is the path.

By now anyone considering all or part of the hike realizes, whether you start humming in the Badlands, crescendo up and over Steens Mountain, chant your way through to Owyhee Canyonlands, or the other way around—at whichever point you begin walking the Oregon Desert Trail, you are guaranteed vistas of canyonlands, gulches, escarpments, playas. You will delight in the new day warble of the meadowlark, the gargle of the raven, the huffing of a startled pronghorn. You will smell the perfume of sage daubed on the wrist of the afternoon after a desert rain and the dank, fecund bouquet rising off the rivers at dusk. That the trail—in fact and in concept—has been introduced sets something in motion, the gentle flap of the butterfly wing that results in a hurricane of change. Imagine the ODT as a slight wave of the hand that ultimately propels the preservation and protection of wild places. Even if you never set foot on the Oregon Desert Trail, it has now been entered and filed in the collective imagination and that it has—it's my opinion—contributes to a greater awareness and general appreciation of the need for wild things and places. That the notion, the concept, of this trail has been brought into existence indelibly shapes our thinking, infiltrates our point of view, regardless of our age or our politics, of which armchair we're expounding from.

The Wilderness Act of 1964 is now in its fifties. Over half a century of action on behalf of wilderness and its preservation. Wilderness historian Dr. Roderick Nash puts the unifying purpose into perspective: "Preserved wilderness is a gesture of restraint on the part of a species notorious for its greed." This notion of restraint that Nash describes, could it be that the inaccessibility and arduousness of this trail is another gesture of restraint, that difficulty of access is a *useful* quality when knighting certain areas as wild and scenic? Could it be that once introduced just the idea of access to "new" wild areas wields an influence that should not be overlooked?

Praise to the gesture and to those who have struggled to articulate it. Curses on the greed. Now we're left to manage, protect, preserve, and it is the job of many. Not of one organization, spokesperson, or perspective but of all. Rationed wilderness. The zoo-ing of the wild, the safari-ing of the pristine. Enough access in a variety of forms to keep us inmates on this crowded planet from starving or rioting.

Enough opportunity to sip the nectar that contact with wild places provides our psyches, but not so much that what is left of the primeval is utterly devastated.

An L. A. Huffman photograph from the late nineteenth century depicts wranglers rounding up wild horses on Montana's eastern grasslands, corralling the bucking, snorting cavvy within a single strand of rope suspended from temporary wooden fence posts: the suggestion of restraint, of corral, of holding, of containment, of restriction. As wild as the horses were, they respected it as though a five-wire fence. The Oregon Desert Trail, all trails, are like a single-strand rope corral, if you will, a metaphor for containment, for respectful conduct within an experience of wild places, preventing us from running willy-nilly through them. It keeps us humans on designated paths, limits the scattering of the seeds of destruction we carry on our soles, within our souls. This desert is a little model of a bigger world. Nature is a mirror of our true nature. What we do or don't do on its behalf is our true nature.

How can we translate our dependence on nature into a respect for nature? Do we truly hold our economic privileges above taking care of the very air that keeps us alive? Is it fair to ask others to bear the burden of our privilege? Is money the only metric with which to measure success? What about environmental measures, ecological measures, sustainability measures? How can the soil of the cultural, corporate, capitalistic message be amended, enriched, altered to grow and sustain different attitudes and philosophies? What can we all agree on? The answers, I believe, lie in science and art and peripheral vision. I believe a kind of sixth sense is necessary. There are instructions waiting in the wings that can get us out of the mess "man-unkind" has created socially and environmentally. It's said if you look to the left or the right of a star you'll see it better. Isn't the same true of problems in general? Even recalcitrant environmental, social, and economic problems? Maybe a more holistic and unbiased view of the challenges before us can return us to being human-kind, get us off our duffs and all wheels back on track.

FIFTEEN

High Road

WHEN THE OREGON Desert Trail was first announced I had the idea, a small undertaking, really, to trace its route from Bend to the Owyhee Canyonlands and address how, by virtue of its twists and turns, it underscored the land-use issues making headlines in the high desert. But thanks to Ammon Bundy's occupation of the Malheur National Wildlife Refuge in 2016, the plot skidded off the road before I even put pen to paper. The foment that surfaced as a result of the occupation was evidence of an anger and unrest that simmered nationwide. What else in this arid place, I wondered, was a poster child for national issues and concerns? As it turns out, a lot of things: water resources, land use, rural-urban divide, pollution, poverty, loss of species, radicalism, racism, environmentalism, natural resource harvest, speculative development. To manage this desert dance, I divided the book into sections and each section into chapters that addressed regional issues and were first cousins to national ones. In the process, many places and people became star players in this odyssey across the Oregon Outback. Both sides of the conflicts proved persuasive, compelling. Indeed, over and again any possibility of a common solution seemed irredeemably high centered. Except when it wasn't. Now that the trail has reached its terminus in the magnificent Owyhee Canyonlands, it's an opportunity to acknowledge models of resolution encountered along the way.

But first, it's back to the Pioneer Saloon in Paisley. One evening several of us artists in residence at PLAYA headed there for a burger. A bunch of Wrangled and cowboy-hatted locals at the bar were playing karaoke, crooning classic country and western songs. "I like all kinds of music . . . country *and* western," snarked one member of the PLAYA contingent, quoting Dolly Parton. After a glass of wine, the PLAYA artists and writers decided to join in, and a competition was underway. The karaoke machine kept score as participants from each team matched skills, artists versus cowboys, urban versus rural. Each performer was boisterously cheered on by their teammates. More beer, more wine. The score was close. The last one to perform was a young screenwriter from Los Angeles. She chose a hip love song. By now the PLAYA team realized that every single word that appeared on the screen had to be sung or points would be lost. She knew the song; was sure she would cinch a perfect score. She didn't anticipate the karaoke version would have miles and miles of "Oh, baby, yes, baby, um baby, feels so good, baby!" at the end. She stood, mortified, looking up at the screen, clutching the microphone, hoping she had just delivered the last line of the refrain when another "oh, baby" would pop up. She was doing her best for the team, putting as much emotion into her delivery as she could muster, singing every word as close to on key as she could manage. At this point, everyone in the whole saloon was cheering her on. When the song finally finished, the score showed the PLAYA team losing, but the victory was in the friendships created. Hokey, I know, but it was true. Common ground was found. The separate lives and differing perspectives discovered that all roads led to a Rome of shared humanity and humor. As *The Ballad of Buster Scruggs* describes, a place we can sing together and get past the meanness of the used-to-be.

And so it is with the examples of successful collaboration encountered while walking the Oregon Desert Trail and the realization we're all in this together, that differing perspectives aren't obstacles, but rather they inform and contribute to solving the challenges. I don't suggest the issues aren't daunting and highly complex. I'm not suggesting karaoke is the way to peace in the world, although the concept is entertaining. But I do suggest that the answers to harder questions are found when we come together as individuals, when a conservationist and a rancher share a flask of whiskey in a pickup while sorting out their differences; not agendas, not political statements, not according to social or cultural caste.

Though much of the ODT requires mapping your own route, along the way we've met individuals and groups successfully creating maps for community-building and consensus as relates to the high desert and, by example, to the region and nation: Alice Elshoff and her rolling-pin protest; the determination of a young Jack Hyde to reverse a rural trend toward poverty bolstered by the commitment and enthusiasm of small-town citizens such as Ginger Casto in Lakeview or Terry Crawford in Christmas Valley; Julie Weikel good-naturedly challenging her neighbor to cross to her side of the street during the protest march in downtown Burns; filmmakers Richard Wilhelm and Sue Arbuthnot creating their insightful and fairhanded documentary *Refuge* about the occupation; the former Harney County sheriff, Dave Ward. Described as "transformative" during the Bundy takeover, Ward was awarded the Center for the American

West's Wallace Stegner Award in 2019, "given to an individual who has made a sustained contribution to the identity of the West." He is in good company, following the likes of documentary filmmaker Ken Burns and author Timothy Egan. There's "Putting the Crook Back in the Crooked River," the initiative launched by ranchers sensitive to the changes in marsh and river health due to commercial demands downriver. And the Roger Worthingtons of the world.

> Look, every day the planet's heating up. Each of us contributes. Some more than others. We need healthy ecosystems throughout the state. Protected public lands support biodiversity. They provide us a place to escape. And (perhaps most importantly) they absorb carbon. By passing laws that set aside public lands, in the fine tradition of Teddy Roosevelt and FDR, we help increase the chance for future generations to live and live well. So, we need more protected places in Oregon, especially in Oregon's high desert. Protect them. Love them. And then leave 'em alone. As my Dad used to say, "sometimes it's best to just leave it where Jesus flang it."

On the occasion of my sixty-fifth birthday I got a lifetime Forest Service park permit, granting me free access to the best of what Jesus flang. When he handed me the permit, the young man in his crisp uniform and Smokey Bear hat smiled and said, "The *pass* will never expire." That smart-aleck Forest Service guy failed to take into account one important fact. It's not just the lifetime park permit that never expires. Neither do I. Neither do you. Our imprint lasts longer than the plastic diapers in the town dump. Seriously, we have to take that imprint seriously. I have come to see my life, all our lives, as part of a linked narrative, like a grove of aspen rhizome-ing its way to eternity. My friend Jan Roberts, named by the Cheyenne in Montana as

Red White Woman in honor of her work with that tribe, explained to me the rhizome-like quality of the Cheyenne view of time. It isn't linear but more like a pond with everything happening on the same surface in the same area. Events are but ripples on the surface. Time is a cycle, like a hoop, a dream catcher. Each stage is a preparation for the next. At the center is timelessness, the eternal present around which the cycles revolve, the cycles of stories, of the journeys of heroes.

Today, there's a growing number of Native American heroes, sung and unsung, who are confidently embracing their rightful place at every table, offering the power of their perspective, their history, their culture, and their understanding of life's cycles. Artist Rick Bartow, who died in 2016, was a member of the Wiyot tribe of Humboldt County in California but made his home in Siletz Indian country on Oregon's coast. Bartow boldly rendered the cultural contradictions he lived on canvas and wood. Though he was the first to point out he was not from a totem pole culture such as those farther up the Northwest coast, the Smithsonian commissioned Bartow to create two columnar sculptures to be installed at the entrance to the American Indian Museum in Washington, DC. *We Were Always Here*, the twenty-foot-tall red cedar pieces, was dedicated in 2012. "It's a cherry on my cake, my big lifetime cake," Bartow said of the installation. "I don't know how it gets bigger than this."

That the First Peoples were always here and always will be is historically and currently a central organizing principle for many tribes. Robert "Bobby" Brunoe, a member of the Confederated Tribes of Warms Springs and the tribes' general manager of natural resources and tribal historic preservation officer explains, "We have a sacred obligation to make sure the Deschutes River is healthy because we will be here forever." This deep spiritual connection to the gifts of the earth informs Brunoe's negotiations between the Confederated Tribes and federal, state, and local agencies. Recently appointed to the High Desert Museum board of directors, he has also served on river conservancy, forestry, watershed, and regional strategies boards and councils. The mood in the natural resources building at Warm Springs is one of organized chaos as input from archaeologists, fire and habitat management specialists, federal agency and conservancy representatives is wrangled into a cohesive proposal or document. As Indian practices and philosophies are better understood, they are increasingly recognized as reinforcing environmental and conservation policies, which, ironically, they always did. "People understand who we are better," says Brunoe. "We take a long view. We are a very patient people so long as the needle is pointed in the right direction. How will we take care of the folks here? Take care of our resources? By planning for the seventh generation as the generations before us did."

The Ashland Shakespeare Festival's commitment to staging new works has resulted in the premiering of plays by Native American playwrights, including *Manhatta*, staged in 2018, a three-way stretch that looked at the contemporary and historical Native American presence in Manhattan, or *Manhatta*, the "land of many hills" as the Lenape people called it. In 2019, *Between Two Knees*, its playwrights an intertribal sketch comedy troupe, made its debut, encouraging the audience to laugh at the worst of the Native American experience, challenging the audience to see it not as a victim story, not as a cautionary tale, but rather as a new American myth.

Returning to her Warm Springs home near Madras, Oregon, in 2019, Elizabeth Woody, former poet laureate of Oregon and an enrolled member of the Confederated Tribes of Warm Springs, is now director of the Warm Springs Museum. Alyssa Macy, COO of the Confederated Tribes of Warm Springs from 2015 through 2019, returned to the reservation after working in advocacy and communications from Wisconsin to Washington, DC. She played a key role in the first-ever United Nations World Conference on Indigenous People held in 2014. In her 2019 commencement speech at Oregon State University–Cascade, Macy began by describing early trauma, cultural shaming, fear, and self-doubt but drew a standing ovation for her concluding statement of strength and determination:

> I took off the stereotypes that I had internalized. The drunk
> Indian, the casino Indian, the uneducated Indian, and more.
> I replaced all of that with the incredible story of resiliency, of
> resistance, the power of culture and language, and the deep con-
> nection to the land and the community. I am not, and never was,
> a Pocahontas Halloween costume or a story of the past. I am of
> the present, and I stand with my ancestors and the sisters that we
> have lost. I am a part of the new Indigenous narrative—rooted,
> thriving, leading, evolving, and building. I am your neighbor and
> we are our future.

ONDA and the Northwest Youth Corps teamed up in the summer of 2019 to create the Tribal Stewards Program with the goal of empowering and inspiring a new generation of high-desert conservationists. The program's first crew represented Warm Springs, Yakama, Wasco, Northern Paiute, Pima, Navajo, and N'chii Wanapum (Columbia River Plateau) tribes. Crew leader Tiyana Casey (N'chii Wanapum) is a college student from Warm Springs, Oregon, studying traditional ecological knowledge—first foods and traditional hunting and gathering techniques, which she wants to share to stabilize young Indigenous people. "I am thrilled," she said, "to have the opportunity to shift my energies to not only land restoration and stewardship but also tie in cultural restoration. My ancestors, family, community, and life experiences have prepared me for seeing the land through the lens that I do."

Don't forget the thru-hikers themselves and the interactions they had with landowners. "This route is expertly put together to highlight land-management tension," says Danny "Caribou" Archibald.

> I can count the number of miles on my hands when there was
> no sign of cows. This was extremely eye opening for me. The
> amount of ranching that goes on in this region, a region I don't
> see renouncing ranching anytime soon, is incredible. In order to
> protect the desert, ONDA is charged with a very difficult task of
> working with ranchers to protect both cows and the land. I think
> that in this very divided country, communication and compromise
> are necessary and ONDA seems to be focusing upon this, which I
> appreciate tremendously. I am certainly inspired by the conversa-
> tions, observations, and thoughts I had on this walk to pursue land
> management negotiations, in hopes of protecting this amazing
> desert as best can be. The creation of a trail by a conservation orga-
> nization is a brilliant way to inspire individuals and create oppor-
> tunities for extremely positive conversations across the route.

"Maybe, as long-distance hikers and adventurers," notes Ryan "Dirt-monger" Sylva, "by spreading the love out just a little bit more, we can be a catalyst in relationships with land management between the right and the left. Here I go associating myself with a group when all I feel is the ultimate connection with the land."

Then there are the groups and organizations that got together to create the Badlands Wilderness Area or the Oregon chapter of the

Dark Sky Initiative. There are the government and private interests that collaborated on the Beatys Butte Wild Horse project. "I love that a few ranchers in the Warner Valley at Adel were able to problem-solve after decades of struggling with the wild-horse populations," says Ginger Casto. "They were able to work with the BLM to bring the herd to a reasonable number and capture, take care of, train, and move those trained horses to new homes in a productive manner."

The importance of the High Desert Museum's constancy and inquisitiveness in the West can't be overstated. Over the course of its nearly forty-year history, the museum has figured out how to walk the tightrope on all sides of the issues. "Creating a place for dialogue begins with creating an experience that reminds people of their common values and vision," says executive director Dana Whitelaw. "The High Desert Museum believes there are core beliefs that enable all humans to connect. With that premise, we create experiences that remind us that we each value beauty, wonder, and a future that holds these values dear. Once we create the platform for presenting how different sides feel, think, and act, we can create connection to our humanity. This is core to creating connection between individuals with differing opinions."

In the Trout Creek Mountains, some of the most secure grazing rights in the West were successfully negotiated. This spawned other, similar successes, notably the groundbreaking 2013 Steens Mountain Comprehensive Recreational Plan that brought all parties to the table and, after five years, to agreement. David Bilyeu of Bend, a member of that team, recalls how the BLM was bullied by everyone. "There was lots of bad blood regarding the BLM when the advisory council first started meeting. But they are not the enemy. They may not always be the best partner, but it's amazing how hard they try. Side boards on every issue to manage. What we rely on the BLM to do is nuts. There are five or six environmental laws that cover every inch of ground." In articulating his philosophical position, Bilyeu says he wants

> better land practices everywhere, for all types: recreationalists, ranchers and everyone concerned. I am not a hardline, no-grazing environmentalist. Good grazing practices can go a long way in correcting some of the imbalances. I have seen work done successfully on the Roaring Springs Ranch, for example, by Stacey Davies, the smartest rancher I know anywhere. My thought was "let's not go to battle over simply the cows on the land, let's go to battle over the quality and condition of the land." All want good stewardship. That was the common place where we all could meet.

"The easy answer is to understand that we all have to listen to people we may not agree with," says Richard Wilhelm. "The High Desert Partnership takes this to heart by inviting former public land policy adversaries to the same table and giving each person a chance to have their voice heard. There are other answers, but this creates an enlightened road map where no single person or group gets to decide where that road leads. It's not purely pragmatic; it relies on both reality and experimentation." The High Desert Partnership (HDP) Wilhelm refers to is increasingly seen as a regional and national model for bringing many opposing views to consensus. Looking for leadership? Don't blame the rural West. Look to it. Formed as a result of the work of the Steens group, HDP describes itself as having been "quietly building a community of resilience and trust that is the bedrock of collaboration" starting well before Ammon Bundy showed up on the scene. Make no mistake, when farmers, ranchers, environmentalists, mineral interests, hunters, Native Americans, wild-horse advocates, BLM, Forest Service, Fish and Wildlife, county and state representatives sit at the same table, odds are the conversation will be a bit tense. Brent Fenty, for one, welcomes this dialogue: "I'm not interested in an echo chamber." The High Desert Partnership has figured out how to accommodate those different perspectives, has mastered patient, respectful ways of creating, as Aldo Leopold said, "thinking community." It is a safe forum in which to "argue like you're right, listen like you're wrong," advocated by Adam Grant of the Wharton School of Business, to listen for the elusive songlines that explain all things, to look for evidence of the *puha* that shapes all things. "It's all about collaboration," says rancher Becky Hyde of her work with conservation groups. "Love is the answer. Getting there is hard."

Hard but essential. Collaboration—not division and rancor—is what will make America and the world great again. George Monibot issues a challenge to us all in his book *Out of the Wreckage: A New Politics for an Age of Crisis.*

> Through restoring community, renewing civic life and claiming our place in the world, we build a society in which our extraordinary nature—our altruism, empathy and deep connection—is released.
>
> When we emerge from an age of loneliness and alienation, from obsession and extreme individualism, from the worship of image and celebrity and power and wealth, we will find a person waiting for us. It is a person better than we might have imagined, whose real character has been surprised. It is the one who lives inside us, who has been there all along.

Because I believe if we go for broke, what we leave for future generations is broken. There's no time for divisiveness, for extreme manifestos. Let's temper the talk of the sixth extinction with "instinction" or "intuition": the result of having seen the problem before and therefore knowing, at some deep level, what to do.

Environmental humanist and philosopher Kathleen Dean Moore posits that "people tend to think they have only two options: hope or despair." But neither, she feels, is acceptable. "Blind hope leads to moral complacency: things will get better, so why should I put myself out? Despair leads to moral abdication: things will get worse no matter what I do, so why should I put myself out?" But between hope and despair, she maintains, is the broad territory of moral integrity. "Even at zero on the hope-o-meter it's still possible to do great work. Even—*especially*—in desperate times, people can make their lives into works of art that embody their deepest values."

After completing the Camino de Santiago and receiving my certificate of pilgrimage in Santiago de Compostela, I continued, as the ancient pilgrims did, to the town of Finisterre, nestled on bluffs overlooking the Atlantic Ocean. The early day penitents christened this town "the end of the Earth" because they believed those bluffs to be exactly that. They would retrieve a scallop shell, the emblem of the camino, and return to their villages with evidence they had stood on the precipice, the brink, looked out across the vast unknowable, stared down the great void. But guess what. The world is not flat.

So, I ask you, what false endings, what false limits of nature, what false limits of our capacity to come together and work out sound solutions do we subscribe to? What social media silos do we hole up in? What cultural dictates do we succumb to that limit our vision, undermine each of our capacities for making positive change? What blinders do we wear? Whether it's Bend's Tours de Coops encouraging backyard farming, Portland's composting project, New York City's wall and rooftop vegetable gardens, Denmark's linked waste-to-energy industries in a perfectly coordinated symbiotic system, or the homes from Nigeria to Mexico lit by Uncharted Play's soccer balls that are designed to gather energy when they're kicked— these are amazing and hopeful and result from a shift in the cultural dialogue, twenty-twenty peripheral vision, and the skills to manifest that vision in the world. What other forces for positive change can we harness locally, globally?

When you cup your hands over these words, pages, chapters, where do you feel the most warmth? I am betting it's the stories, the anecdotes. Listening to, seeing the person across the table as an aspect of yourself, there's the rub and the answer. During the second half of life, according to author James Hollis, the focus changes from the external—what does the world ask of me as professional, partner, parent?—to an inside job: What question do I answer with my life? Each of us, according to Hollis, is a crucial part of a great unfolding. Something is living us more than we are living it. We don't create ourselves; we happen to ourselves. We don't make our story; our story makes us. As W. H. Auden wrote: "We are lived by powers we pretend to understand." The common denominator for a tenable future requires staying at the table until we discover our shared humanity. Don't take your life personally, take it to the limit.

To heal the effects of the Bundy occupation and the rude desecration of the refuge headquarters, Bend residents Jay Bowerman and his wife, Teresa, turned to music, commissioning a symphony as salve, as blessing. They enlisted Chris Thomas, a young and accomplished Los Angeles–based composer who spent hours in the refuge, recording the wind and the birdcall, turning those sounds into orchestration. In May of 2019 I drove to Burns for the premiere. It was held in the high school gym. Banners extolling the Burns Highlanders were suspended from the rafters, the school slogan of "Let fear be far from all" was painted in large letters across the cement block wall. It was in that very gym in 2016 that rancorous meetings between area residents, law enforcement, federal government representatives, and the Bundy contingent took place. At the time there was no sign of any willingness to turn swords into plowshares. The world was flat.

But on the afternoon of the premiere, the world was round, the gym was filled (estimated five hundred in attendance) with a very different energy. The audience included old and young, farmers, business owners, ranchers, local officials, Paiutes from the nearby Burns Paiute reservation, busloads of Bendites, fathers in John Deere caps with children in tow, little girls in princess dresses, a poet from nearby Hines who leaves poems in ziplock bags along the town's walking trail for people to take and enjoy.

The Central Oregon Symphony musicians from Bend, clad formally in black dresses or tuxedos, tuned their instruments; the cacophony like the squabbling and squawking of a flock of cranes coming in for a landing. The Harney County judge welcomed everyone. Maestro Michael Gesme, conductor of the Central Oregon Symphony, came onstage, took the baton in hand, and raised it into the air. A live recording of the song of the red-winged blackbird opened the symphony. Soon violin and cello began to weave their way in, unobtrusively, seamlessly. The movements evoked the early formation of the Malheur Basin, offered a musical tribute to the Paiute, visited the darker chapters in Malheur history, celebrated the birds of the refuge, and concluded with an uplifting musical fanfare, a toast to the future of the region. When it was over, everyone jumped to their feet, whistling and cheering. "True art appeals to our humanity," Chris Thomas said. "It has the power to heal and connect us, to move us from focusing on our differences, toward what we have in common."

It is now to each of us to create movement and momentum toward commonality, to perceive what is, and smartly inform what will be, and in so doing make sure this desert, this region, this nation, this world can continue to ask the questions worth asking, to seek the answers worth seeking. For those of us who love the Oregon Outback, it is up to us to shape and ensure the future of all that the high desert embraces—critters, people, magical places—so those who follow can also rejoice in earth's bold collision with sky, the iridescence of the raven feather, the magnificent canvas of the Great Basin. We must think like an otter, an owl, a lily, a lupine, think like a sawyer, an eagle, a Paiute, a settler, a cowboy, a canyon, so those following can discern the faint contrails of our triumphs and tragedies, of the right work we accomplished writ across this scape. And within those chalky tracings, next generations can inscribe their own stories of what's best for most. We'll do this, of course we will, and so will those who follow because it's the meet and right thing to do. And just watch this straight-faced desert crack a smile of deep gratitude.

ACKNOWLEDGMENTS

I extend my deepest thanks to all my trail angels—colleagues, teachers, mentors, friends, and family—who helped this book with their genius and generosity, comment and critique: Ginger Casto, Joanne Diepenheim, Carolyn Dufurrena, Alice Elshoff, Dagmar Eriksson, Stu Garrett, Louise Hawker, Sue Hollern, Becky Hyde, Patty Limerick, Kathleen Dean Moore, Kent Nelson, Sally Russell, Julie Weikel, and Dana Whitelaw.

Special acknowledgment and thanks to those who read and responded to early drafts and pointed me toward important resources: Dave Bilyeu, Brent Fenty, Bill Marlett, Renee Patrick, Bill and Trish Smith, and Sam Waterston.

To the guardians of the night sky: Richard Berry, William Kowalik, Dr. Alton Luken, and Roger Worthington.

To my children, Elise, Eben, and Katharine Bartow, and my daughter-in-law, Yusselly.

To documentary filmmakers Sue Arbuthnot and Richard Wilhelm for making *Refuge*.

To archaeologist Dr. Dennis Jenkins who puts our insignificance into such jolly perspective.

To the thru-hikers who travel the pages of this book: Heather "Anish" Anderson, Danny "Caribou" Archibald, Sage Clegg, Bob

"Huck Finn" Jessee, Mary "Fireweed" Kwart, Ryan "Dirtmonger" Sylva.

To graphic artist Greg Cross for so deftly capturing the Oregon Desert Trail in map form.

To Scott Nelson, whose cover image inspired people to pick up and peruse the book.

To portrait photographer Marina Koslow Davis for making me look good.

To PLAYA and its founders, Bill Roach and Julie Bryant, and to the Spring Creek Project's Cabin at Shot Pouch Creek for providing retreat and inspiration during the process of imagining and creating this book.

To everyone at the University of Washington Press, especially Andrew Berzanskis, senior acquisitions editor, for his persistence, patience, energy, and skill; Julie Fergus, director of marketing and sales, for helping spread the word; Regan Huff, formerly senior acquisitions editor, for giving the original proposal for this book a thumbs-up; and copy editor Joeth Zucco for her rigorous attention to every word, sentence, paragraph, and page.

To the University of Washington Press for standing by this project.

To Chuck McGrath for many insightful conversations about the direction of this book.

And finally, to all who dearly love a place and are committed to its care.

SELECTED READING

Binkovitz, Leah. "A Pair of Monumental Sculptures Makes Its Way to American Indian Museum," *Smithsonian.com*, September 5, 2012, https://www.smithsonianmag.com/smithsonian-institution/a-pair-of-monumental-sculptures-makes-its-way-to-american-indian-museum-26023025/.

Bird, Anna. "Painting Big in the Playa." *1859 Oregon's Magazine*, July 1, 2016.

Bishop, Ellen Morris. *In Search of Ancient Oregon: A Geological and Natural History*. New York: Workman Press, 2006.

Catton, William. *Overshoot, The Ecological Basis of Revolutionary Change*. Champaign: University of Illinois Press, 1982.

Chatwin, Bruce. *The Songlines*. New York: Penguin Books, 1988.

Diehl, Caleb. "Walking on a Knife's Edge." *Oregon Business*, November 12, 2018, https://www.oregonbusiness.com/article/energy-environment/item/18574-walking-on-a-knife-s-edge.

Douglas, William O. *My Wilderness: The Pacific West*. New York: Doubleday, 1960.

Ferguson, Denzel, and Nancy Ferguson. *Sacred Cows at the Public Trough*. Bend, OR: Maverick Publications, 1983.

Forbes, Peter. *Conservation for a New Generation: Redefining Natural Resources Management*. Washington, DC: Island Press, 2002.

Gray, Edward. *William "Bill" W. Brown, 1855–1941: Legend of Oregon's High Desert*. Salem, OR: Your Town Press, 1993.

Griffin, Donald. *Animal Minds: Beyond Cognition to Consciousness*. Chicago: University of Chicago Press, 1992.

Hanson, Thor. *Feathers: The Evolution of a Natural Miracle*. New York: Basic Books, 2011.

Jackman, E. R., and John Scharff. *Steens Mountain: In Oregon's High Desert Country*. Caldwell, ID: Caxton Press, 1967.

Jackman, E. R., and R. A. Long. *The Oregon Desert*. Caldwell, ID: Caxton Press, 1964.

Kearney, Ryan. "White People Love Hiking. Minorities Don't. Here's Why." *New Republic*, updated July 13, 2015, https://newrepublic.com/article /114621/national-parks-popular-white-people-not-minorities-why.

Ketcham, Christopher. "Taming the Wilderness." *Orion Magazine*, August 4, 2014, https://orionmagazine.org/article/taming-the-wilderness/.

Keyser, James. *Indian Rock Art of the Columbia Plateau*. Seattle: University of Washington Press, 1992.

Kimmerer, Robin Wall. *Gathering Moss: A Natural and Cultural History of Mosses*. Corvallis: Oregon State University Press, 2003.

Krutch, Joseph Wood. *The Desert Year*. Iowa City: University of Iowa Press, 2010.

Lamm, Richard. *The Angry West: A Venerable Land and Its Future*. Boston: Houghton Mifflin, 1982.

Leopold, Aldo. *Sand County Almanac*. New York: Oxford University Press, 1949.

Li, Qing. *Forest Bathing: How Trees Can Help You Find Health and Happiness*. New York: Viking, 2018.

Limerick, Patty. "Let's Ask American Indians about the 'Immigration Crisis,'" *Denver Post*, updated February 1, 2017. https://www.denverpost.com/2017 /01/14/lets-ask-american-indians-about-the-immigration-crisis/.

Litesmith. "Trail Lingo." Accessed April 12, 2019. https://www.litesmith.com /trail-lingo/.

Louv, Richard. *Last Child in the Woods: Saving Our Children from Nature-Deficit Disorder*. Chapel Hill, NC: Algonquin Books, 2005.

Macfarlane, Robert. *The Old Ways: A Journey on Foot*. New York: Penguin, 2012.

Matteson, Mollie, and George Wuerthner. *Welfare Ranching: The Subsidized Destruction of the American West*. Washington, DC: Island Press, 2002.

Monibot, George. *Out of the Wreckage: A New Politics for an Age of Crisis*. New York: Verso Books, 2017.

Moore, Kathleen Dean, and Michael P. Nelson. *Moral Ground: Ethical Action for a Planet in Peril*. San Antonio: Trinity University Press, 2011.

Morrell, Virginia. *Animal Wise: The Thoughts and Emotions of Our Fellow Creatures*. New York: Broadway Books, 2014.

Nash, Roderick Frazier. *Wilderness and the American Mind*. New Haven, CT: Yale University Press, 1982.

Obama, Michelle. *Becoming*. New York: Crown Publishing Group, 2018.

Oregon Natural Desert Association. *Oregon Desert Trail Guidebook*. https:// onda.org/regions/oregon-desert-trail/.

———. "Tribal Stewards Program Provides Career Mentorship." July 2017. https://onda.org/2019/07/tribal-stewards-program/.

Pray, Alice Day. *A Homesteader's Portfolio: The Memoir of a Single Woman Homesteader*. Corvallis: Oregon State University Press, 1993.

Preston, Douglas. "The Day the Dinosaurs Died." *New Yorker*, April 8, 2019. https://www.newyorker.com/magazine/2019/04/08/the-day-the-dinosaurs-died.

Pyle, Robert Michael. *Wintergreen: Listening to the Land's Heart*. Boston: Houghton Mifflin, 1998.

Quartz, Alissa. *Squeezed: Why Our Families Can't Afford America*. New York: Ecco Press, 2018.

Ragen, Brooks. *The Meek Cutoff: Tracing the Oregon Trail's Lost Wagon Train of 1845*. Seattle: University of Washington Press, 2017.

Richard, Terry. "Desert Trail Showcases an Often Unseen Side of Oregon." *Oregonian*, October 14, 2012.

SOURCE Weekly Woman of the Year edition. "Alice Elshoff." May 2016.

Spurr, Kyle. "Preserving Memories of Millican." *Bulletin*, April 4, 2019.

Stauffer, Charles W. *Homesteading the High Desert: Oregon's Lost Creek Valley, 1910 to 1920*. Marylhurst, OR: Marylhurst College, 1988.

Stegner, Wallace. *Where the Bluebird Sings to Lemonade Springs: Living and Writing in the West*. New York: Penguin Books, 1992.

Wewa, Wilson. *Legends of the Northern Paiute*. Corvallis: Oregon State University Press, 2017.

Winch, Martin T. *Tumalo, Thirsty Land: History of Tumalo Irrigation District*. Portland: Oregon Historical Society, 1985.

Witty, Jim. *Meet Me in the Badlands: Exploring Central Oregon*. Bend, OR: Published by Friends and Family of Jim Witty, 2009.

ABOUT THE AUTHOR

Award-winning high-desert writer Ellen Waterston has published two books of literary nonfiction and four books of poetry. Her most recent collection of poetry, *Hotel Domilocos*, was published in 2017. She adapted her verse novel, *Vía Láctea*, to a libretto, which premiered in 2016 as a full-length opera and is slated for a second staging in 2021. *Where the Crooked River Rises*, a collection of award-winning essays, was published in 2010. Her work has also appeared in a wide variety of journals, magazines, and anthologies.

A strong champion of the literary arts, Waterston founded and for over a decade directed The Nature of Words, a literary nonprofit. She is the founder and president of the Waterston Desert Writing Prize, awarded annually to nonfiction projects concerning deserts, and in 2000 she founded the Writing Ranch, which specializes in workshops and retreats for emerging and established writers. In recognition of her work as an author and literary arts advocate, she received an honorary doctorate in Humane Letters from Oregon State University–Cascades. Waterston has been awarded numerous fellowships, grants, and residencies. She is a WILLA and *Foreword Reviews* finalist in literary nonfiction and a two-time WILLA award winner in poetry and the winner of the Obsidian Prize in Poetry. A former rancher, she lives in central Oregon's high desert.